# Escape
## from the
# Rocking
## Chair

# ABRAHAM GUERRERO

**TRIUNFO.**
PUBLICACIONES

**Proofreading:**
Leroy Ramos, Natalia Soriano, and Axel C. Orellana (Spanish version)
Richard Mohammed, Rubén Feliciano, and Dr. Bruce Bauer (English version)

**Layout, interior and cover design:** Axel C. Orellana

**Additional resources for cover and back cover:** Rocking chair (by Valery Sibrikov / Bigstockphoto.com), table and laptop (by Zan / ninetofive.me), woman in rocking chair (by Svetlana Radayeva / Bigstockphoto.com), wooden floor and autumn background (by Valentin Agapov / Bigstockphoto.com), author's profile picture (by Axel Orellana), iPad (by Tanya / dribble.com/lazycrazy), hands (by PSDCovers.com).

**Images from Bigstockphoto.com:** Page 1 (by Valery Sibrikov), p. 9 (by JCPJR), p. 10 (by Stéphane Bidouze), p. 14 (by RVLSOFT), p. 17 (by Glenda Powers), p. 18 (by Ieva Geneviciene), p. 22 (by Kamira), p. 27 (by Attila Barabas), p. 28 (by Alan and Vicena Poulson), p. 30 (by AnnekaS), p. 31 (by TCEY), p. 32 (by Aleksandr Lychagin), p. 35 (by Konstantin Kirillov), p. 37 (by Ilja Mašík), p. 40 (by TCEY), p. 43 (by Denis Pepin), p. 45 (by Mike Kiev), p. 47 (Edhar Yuualaits), p. 53 (by Subbotina Anna), p. 54 (by Jasmin Merdan), p. 58 (by Edyta Pawlowska), p. 63 (by Lev Dolgachov), p. 65 (by George Muresan), p. 69 (by Pics Five), p. 73 (by Tom Wang), p. 77 (by Sergey Nivens), p. 85 (Federico Caputo), p. 87 (by Tyler Olson), p. 88 (M. Sørensen), p. 89 (by Viktor Levi), p. 91 (by Patrick Miko), p. 95 (by Mehmet Dilsiz), p. 96 (by Cathy Yeulet), p. 101 (by Aaron Amat Zaragoza), p. 103 (by Dmitriy Shironosov), p. 104 (by Khakimullin Aleksandr), p. 109 (by Ben Goode), p. 114 (by Gino Santa Maria), p. 123 (by Mike_Kiev), p. 125 (by Radu Razvan), p. 127 (by M Sørensen), p. 128 (PHOTOMORPHIC PTE. LTD.), rocking chair featured at the top of each odd page (by Valery Sibrikov), and dog with books featured in the application questions at the end of each chapter (by Javier Brosch).

**Other images:** By Pixeden.com (iPad at the beginning of each chapter, as well as in pp. 20, 48), by Tanya - www.dribble.com/lazycrazy (p. 124), and by PSDCovers.com (p. 118).

**Executive Production:** José A. Regús

Triunfo Publicaciones, Inc.
P.O. BOX 451351
Kissimmee, FL 34744
USA

ISBN 0-9905774-0-6

Printed in the United States of America.

# A few words of encouragement...

*Escape from the Rocking Chair* is a frank analysis of mission and structure in the Seventh-day Adventist Church. It offers an approach that we would do well in applying, so that mission continues to be the core motive of what we are and do.

> **– Dr. Jorge Mayer,** *vice-president. Southern Union Conference of the Seventh-day Adventist Church.*

This book is a fearless cry on the church's danger of institutionalization... Reading it will help the church rethink the purpose of its existence. The church emerged in the context of Revelation 12 with the mission of proclaiming the everlasting Gospel, and if we fail to fulfill our mission we also lose the purpose of our existence. The moment we forget about mission we'll be placing a knife on our neck, right on the jugular.

> **– Dr. Alejandro Bullón,** *church leader, evangelist and prolific writer.*

Abraham Guerrero's work is both provocative and affirming. It challenges all of us who love the church to be strongly supportive of who we are and where we are going while at the same time daring to ask if we can do better. It calls us to have a healthy sense of dissatisfaction not with the church per se, but with the level of success we are experiencing on all fronts.

> **– Dr. Barry Oliver,** *president. South Pacific Division of the Seventh-day Adventist Church.*

This book by Dr. Guerrero is simply exceptional. It shows a great respect for the church and yet the author dares to ask really tough, important questions. Every single page is a drop of eye salve by which God can anoint our eyes so we can see how much we need to bring mission back to the front seat in everything we do, both as a church and individually.

> **– Dr. Allan Machado,** *vice-president. Florida Conference of Seventh-day Adventists.*

Several people and even churches make the mistake of confusing motion with progress. This book teaches the main key for really effective work.

*- Pr. Roger Hernández, ministerial director and evangelist. Southern Union of Seventh-day Adventists.*

Can the continuation of the same approach ever accomplish the task the Church faces in reaching unreached people with the Good News? *Escape from the Rocking Chair* asks probing questions concerning Adventist mission that require hard answers..

*- Dr. Bruce Bauer, director. Department of World Mission, Andrews University.*

Few books I have read over the last several years have as clearly identified both the problem and the solution to the current needs of the church as this one. If you seek to understand the mission of the church—read this book. If you seek to understand the purpose of church structure—read this book. Most of all, if you seek to understand the mission of the Lord God for your life—read this book..

*- Pr. Thomas Lemon, president. Mid-America Union Conference of Seventh-day Adventists.*

This should be a reference book for all church leaders who want to foster spiritual revival. .

*- Pr. Mario Niño, associate stewardship director. General Conference of Seventh-day Adventists.*

This book challenges our organizational pride and at the same time it instills a deep respect for the church. It gives you a close-up look of the problem, just like when a surgeon spots a malignant, end-stage tumor on a patient's organ. But it takes the tumor out!!

*- Pr. Reymer Sánchez, president. North Western Venezuelan Region of Seventh-day Adventists.*

As a church we run the risk of being overtaken by comfort-seeking, being distracted with irrelevant activities, or losing a clear notion of our priority. In *Escape from the Rocking Chair*, Dr. Guerrero brings back the right focus and reinforces the need to concentrate all our strength in fulfilling mission.

*- Pr. Erton Köhler, president. South American Division of the Seventh-day Adventist Church.*

# TABLE OF CONTENTS

# DEDICATION

To God, for He has forgiven me every time I've failed, and He loves me in spite of my failures. Thank you Lord!

To my wife Natalia, my parents Gustavo and Delis, my brother Gustavo and my sister Dellys, my children Ángel and Natasha. I'd like to see you guys among the redeemed people when Jesus finishes this mission for our salvation.

To the church board members in all Adventists congregations, their local pastors, church leaders at the Conference/Mission, Union, and General Conference levels. May the Lord always provide for people like Aaron and Hur to hold your arms in prayer and support.

# ACKNOWLEDGMENTS

To Dr. Bruce Bauer, who offered his support and guidance for me even in the early stages of this process.

To people such as Dr. Allan Machado, Dr. Barry Oliver, Dr. Cheryl Doss, Dr. Jorge Mayer, Pr. Reymer Sánchez, Pr. Roger Hernández, Pr. Mario Niño, Pr. Leroy Ramos, Dr. Michael Cauley, Pr. Thomas Lemon, Dr. George Knight and Pr. Alfredo Campechano, among others, for their selfless support and valuable ideas.

# FOREWORD

Too many people confuse motion with progress and progress with success. Confronting such misconceptions forms the foundation of Abraham Guerrero's *Escape from the Rocking Chair: Breaking the Cycle of Oscillation between success and failure in your Life and in the Church*.

The only genuine success, he points out, arrives with the second advent of Jesus. In the meantime, all our ingenuity and energy needs to be focused on the church's one mission: Spreading the biblical message to all the world in preparation for that great day.

Unfortunately, it is all too easy for the church to put forth massive energy without making much progress, which Guerrero nicely illustrates with his rocking chair motif. Some, he notes, have recognized the problem but have come to the wrong solution. The answer is not ceasing to support the church but to encourage and help it to continually refocus on its unique and singular all-important mission.

*Escape from the Rocking Chair* is a provocative discussion of a topic that should continually be at the forefront of Adventist thinking. The book not only raises the problems involved but also points toward workable solutions. Not the least of its contributions is a thoughtful and balanced discussion of the relationship between the organized church and supportive independent ministries.

Guerrero does not claim to have all of the answers. And some of his readers might have ideas that differ from his. If so, let's hear them. What is most important is not agreement or disagreement but transforming the work of Adventism from motion to a genuine progress that moves us rapidly toward the fulfilment of mission. It is in that context that I highly recommend *Escape from the Rocking Chair* for all who are concerned with world mission and the message of the three angels. The book is a stimulant to both thought and discussion on the most important topic in Adventism. You cannot help but think about how to do mission better as you read this helpful volume.

**Dr. George R. Knight**
*Professor Emeritus of Church History,*
*Andrews University.*

I WAS sitting on a rocking chair, with my fingers on the laptop. Then I started typing, "What is the church here for?" In my mind, that was a very easy question. Well, at least that's what I thought until I saw Tom's response via Internet, "The church is here to meet my needs!"

Can you imagine what would happen if in the church we try to meet the needs and satisfy the desires of everyone? In a sarcastic but very realistic manager-pastor comparison, somebody listed a few things he would do to drive a business manager up the wall and lead them to failure:

> "I'd make him responsible for the success of an organization but give him no authority. I'd provide him with unclear goals, ones the organization didn't completely agree to. I'd ask him to provide a service of an ill-defined nature, apply a body of knowledge having few absolutes and staff his organization with only volunteers who donated just a few hours a week at the most. I'd expect him to work 10 to 12 hours per day and have his work evaluated by a committee of 300 to 500 amateurs. I'd call him minister and make him accountable to God."[1]

Without question, pastors and other church leaders have to cope with their own dose of pressure as they perform their duties. I very much enjoy being a pastor, though. But I've had that privilege for long enough to realize it is difficult to take the church where you think you should take it, especially when everybody pushes or pulls in a different direction.

If pastors or other leaders guide the church to focus on serving the poor, they may face criticism for being on the "social gospel" side, supposedly ignoring the preaching of the "present truth;" if their emphasis is mainly on preaching rather than on social action, then they are seen as ignoring the needy. If the preaching condemns sin, some would think it is too aggressive; if it doesn't, then it lacks boldness.

If the church has a big budget for evangelism, some would complain that many other needs are being neglected; if the budget is adapted to the needs of all church programs, departments, and people, some would obviously argue that the church is not using enough money for evangelism, and that therefore mission is being dangerously disregarded. If you don't preach and teach about health reform, some would say you're ignoring "the right hand of the work;" but guess what? If you talk about the subject, then you run into the danger of being labeled as a dissident!

But problems do not end there. If those who organize music buy into the contemporary trend towards worshipping at the beat of drums, with electric guitars, and other instruments, some would wage war against church leaders for not being courageous enough to "stop worldly influences from contaminating the church;" if they keep away from percussion, the electrifying jingle of contemporary guitars, and the fast-paced tunes that attract younger generations, then some would say the church is frozen in time.

A few years after being assigned to his congregation, when the pastor finally thinks he has some idea of the direction where to lead the church that's been placed under his leadership, then he's notified he will be moved to another church or district. Then, mysteriously, some of the plans and perspectives that seemed so deeply rooted in the church suddenly disappear when the new pastor arrives with his own perspective and his new plans.

The list of issues could go on and on. As a result, many churches swing from one issue to the next and from one side of the discussion to the opposite, just like rocking chairs rock back and forth. In the meantime, pastors and churchgoers quietly watch the pendulum come and go, time and time again.

Bob Roberts observed in another context that "we have segmented and compartmentalized the different dimensions of the church and thereby failed to understand its function in terms of the whole."[2] The church's youth director insists that his department needs more money than the other ones because it's in the young years when most of the decisions to accept Christ as Savior are usually made, but the Sabbath School director argues that her department is "the heart of the Church," and therefore it should receive privileged attention. All other department leaders have a similar theory, and end up pulling time, people, and resources towards their own department's plans.

Way too often, one agenda item is conflicting with another, and it is almost impossible for all activities to fit in the church's calendar and for the church budget to provide for everything. Sometimes, instead of the Sabbath being truly a day of rest, Saturday looks more like the most stressful day of the week.

In a research project related to mission strategy, Juan Caicedo interviewed a number of Adventist pastors in his field. Most of them expressed their conviction that the church exists to bring others to Christ and disciple them so they can do the same thing with others. Interestingly, however, many of these pastors complained that they face too many and very different expectations in ministry. Although pastors' daily agenda and their church's schedule may be already full to overflowing, emergencies surface very frequently. As a result, pastors generally have to adjust their plans according to the need of the moment, often at the expense of what they really want to accomplish for the church's success in mission.[3]

In 2011, when G. T. Ng presented his Secretary's Report to the Annual Council of the Seventh-day Adventist Church, he explained in slide 33 of his PowerPoint presentation that as the church grows, it tends to become institutionalized, to spend more resources on baptized membership than on mission, and while "mission is not forgotten," it is "sidelined amidst pressing demands of programs and institutions."[4]

The Seventh-day Adventist Church as a worldwide organization has experienced such swinging too: Instead of celebrating success as the denomination marked its 150th anniversary, world church president Ted Wilson said in 2013 that such milestone was actually "a very sad anniversary," because "we should have been home by now!"[5] Founders of Adventism didn't really want to establish a denomination, and would be surprised to come across the huge organization that has resulted from their efforts.

George Knight aptly explains the paradox by saying that Adventism "began aggressively antiorganizational, but today it is the most highly structured church in the history of Christianity."[6] In that respect, Adventists' attitudes towards organizational structure have shown a behavior that is very similar to that of my grandpa's rocking chair. And it appears that this rocking chair is going back towards an aggressive antiorganizational attitude, because many have recently expressed their criticism about church structure in such loud and clear voices that perhaps would have probably been impossible to imagine fifty years ago.

Yes, in many ways, the church behaves like a rocking chair. However, I wouldn't simply close my eyes and blame church leaders. If the church has been behaving this way, it is in response to the needs and pressures of members, those who make decisions or push them in committees at different levels.[7] Bruce Bauer highlights Stanley Mooneyham's statement that church structures "tend to be run on the consensus of a large number of Christians with wide ranges of commitment and differing understanding of the mission of the church," and that "consequently, such structures tend to be impotent in the face of situations that require a prophetic stance."[8] Although Bauer insists on the fact that this very structure which is slow and ponderous also "gives the church continuity and follow-through," he admits that such a problem often leads "to waste, inefficiency and bureaucracy."[9]

A very significant danger when analyzing these situations is that your words can easily be misinterpreted as rebellious and you might be labeled as separatist. It happened in my case. It looks like it was yesterday afternoon to me. I was finishing up my bachelor in theology, and one day a prominent church leader approached me, evidently surprised that I wanted to be an Adventist pastor.

—So, did your dad quit being a dissident?—he bluntly asked me.

I know, my dad has always been open to recognize failures within the organizational system of the Adventist church. But ever since I can remember he's loved the church so much that he usually gets in serious trouble for defending the church from separatist movements. Unfortunately, some people think that if you openly talk about a problem in the church's structure or regarding a particular leader, you will probably be willing to leave the church and join or start another organization. At least in what respects to me and my dad, nothing can be farther away from reality.

But we are not the only ones who have been misunderstood in that respect. Anyone who talks about problems related to the church, its structure, or its leaders, runs into the danger of been labeled as someone who is against the church.

In 2001, George Knight published a book entitled *Organizing to Beat the Devil,* in which he ably analyzed the historical development of the Seventh-day Adventist Church's structure. In 2004, the book was reprinted under a new title, and the differences between the first and second editions are quite revealing in this respect.

What really grabbed my attention the most in the second edition was the postscript. According to what the author himself explains in that section, some of Knight's arguments in the book were misunderstood as if the author were saying that church structure should be thrown away. In 2004, a particular church planter (until then a well-recognized leader employed by the denomination) somehow concluded that "there were better ways to do mission than through the Seventh-day Adventist organizational structure,"[10] so he quit his job as a pastor and decided to start a new organization.

One of the things he did afterwards was contacting George Knight to request his support, inferring from the reading of his book that the author would support a separatist endeavor. In the second edition, Knight decided to make things as clear as possible: he would not support such a thing.

If anyone concludes, after reading this book, that church structure is the problem and that the solution is either to join a separatist independent movement or to create one, they are misinterpreting my arguments and need to read the book again from cover to cover. The only purpose of this book is to highlight the need to better align our church's structure—and the structure

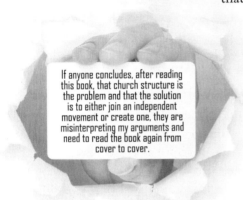

If anyone concludes, after reading this book, that church structure is the problem and that the solution is to either join an independent movement or create one, they are misinterpreting my arguments and need to read the book again from cover to cover.

of our own life—with mission, which is the reason for our existence.

Jesus was in direct opposition to the type of criticism which is focused on someone else's mistakes while ignoring one's own problems. The best way to help correct any imperfections in others is by reforming our own life. Jesus Christ put it this way:

Do not judge, or you too will be judged. For in the same way you judge others, you will be judged, and with the measure you use, it will be measured to you. Why do you look at the speck of sawdust in your brother's eye and pay no attention to the plank in your own eye? How can you say to your brother, "Let me take the speck out of your eye," when all the time there is a plank in your own eye? You hypocrite, first take the plank out of your own eye, and then you will see clearly to remove the speck from your brother's eye (Matthew 7:1-5).

Welcome to the study adventure in which, by God's grace, we will find solution to these issues. The next few chapters are designed to help us "take the plank out" of our own eye, so we can then improve any imperfections that there might be in others, or in the church as an organization. True, there are evils in the Seventh-day Adventist Church, and there will always be. But the church, though enfeebled and defective as it is, and even "needing to be reproved, warned, and counseled, is the only object upon earth upon which Christ bestows His supreme regard."[11] God has a solution at hand for the church's structural problems. And perhaps some of us will be surprised to realize that the same solution is available to fix our own problems of oscillation between success and failure. Let's explore it together!

**THINK-IT-THROUGH AND APPLICATION QUESTIONS**

1. In this chapter it is stated that "it is difficult to take the church where you think you should take it, especially when everybody pushes or pulls in a different direction" (p.9). Would you agree or disagree? How would you explain it?

........................................................................................

........................................................................................

........................................................................................

2. What do you think of Jesus' words in Matthew 7:1-5?

..............................................................................................................

..............................................................................................................

..............................................................................................................

3. Tom said, "The church is here to meet my needs!" How would you help Tom better understand the church's mission?

..............................................................................................................

..............................................................................................................

..............................................................................................................

## References for this chapter

[1] James Hamilton. Quoted in H.B. London and Neil B. Wiseman, *Pastors at Greater Risk* (Ventura, CA: Regal Books, 2003), 64.

[2] Bob Roberts. *Transformation: How glocal churches transform lives and the world.* (Grand Rapids, MI: Zondervan, 2006), 26.

[3] Juan Caicedo. Audio Interviews presented at Andrews University for the class Strategies for World Mission, June 2013.

[4] G.T. Ng, "Membership Dilemma: Promise and Peril, Secretary's report to the Annual Council", General Conference of Seventh-day Adventists, Silver Spring, MD, 2011. Slide 33.

[5] Mark Kellner, "'No more anniversaries,' Wilson says in Spring Meeting sermon", http://news.adventist.org/en/archive/articles/2013/04/14/no-mo-re-anniversaries-wilson-says-in-spring-meeting-sermon (accessed July 7, 2013).

[6] George Knight, "Organizing for Mission: The Development of Seventh-day Adventist Organizational Structure", http://www.adventist.org/world-church/commission-ministries-services-structures/knight-organized-for-mission.pdf (accessed July 7, 2013), p. 1.

[7] Bruce L. Bauer, "Congregational and Mission Structures and How the Seventh-day Adventist Church Has Related to Them" (D.Miss. dissertation, Fuller Theological Seminary, School of World Mission, 1983), 234.

[8] Ibid, 15.

[9] Ibid., 15, 16.

[10] George R. Knight. (2006). *Organizing for Mission and Growth: The Development of Adventist Church Structure.* Hagerstown, MD: Review and Herald Publishing Association, p. 182.

[11] Ellen White. *Testimonies to ministers,* p. 49.

# MY GRANDPA'S ROCKING CHAIR

I MET Elizabeth when I was about to step into the water in a nearby river to officiate a baptismal ceremony. She had felt called by God to get baptized on that day, but she also felt her church's members were not going to allow her to be baptized again.

—Why?—I asked her.

Her eyes were full of sadness when she told me she had accepted Jesus early in her teenage years and had been baptized, but one day she slipped away from church and away from God out of curiosity for parties and all the other stuff that comes with them. However, she returned a few years later and was baptized again, sincerely intending to stay in Jesus's arms forever. But she fell into sin again and left the church once more, only to realize later that she needed to return. This happened six times, until that day by the river.

—Can you understand my problem now?—she asked me as her eyes were already full with tears and as I saw the drops slide down her cheeks— Who in the world is going to believe I really want to follow Jesus now?

Now, this is for you, the reader. Have you ever sat in a rocking chair? I love sitting down and closing my eyes while I feel the relaxing movement forward and backward. But in spiritual life, moving back and forth like a rocking chair is simply frustrating. When facing an endless series of triumphs and defeats, sometimes it seems that it will not be possible to get anywhere. Sadly, Elizabeth is not the only one who suffers as she swings back and forth in life's rocking chair. Too many people go from failure to what seems to be success, but then back to failure, as if it were imperative to repeat the cycle again and again.

## A sad reality

At the end of every year (and in other special occasions), millions of people make resolutions that during the following year, finally, they will achieve those goals they have always dreamed about: to stop worrying so much, to keep their expenses within budget, to spend some time every day in good reading, to exercise three times a week, to minimize T.V. time, to save enough for the down payment of a new house or fix their credit score, to organize their time more carefully, to get out of debt, to quit that bad habit nobody knows about but themselves, to pray before every meal, to wake up a little earlier so there's time to read the Bible... The list could be endless.

*New Years Resolution List*
*Get organised*
*STOP smoking*
*Find a job*
*LOSE 20 pounds*
*10 pounds*
*5 pounds*

But it is difficult to achieve our goals, especially if they are really significant. It would be wonderful to be able to honestly say life is easy to tackle with, and that it does not have very many challenges. I would love to write here that human beings are able to achieve what they aim at without too many problems, but that would be a sheer lie!

Almost anyone who has tried to change a habit or to give up a long-cherished sin knows how hard it is. It feels like our own brain is waging war against us. "We say we're going to change, we may even do it for a little while, but soon we find ourselves back to our old habits."[1] Some even achieve their goals for some brief time: they start minimizing worries, spending more time with God, being more careful with their expenses, reading a little bit every day, exercising, and the like. But unfortunately after some time the power of our good intentions seems to fade away in the midst of the pressures of our old habits.

## Learning from a little puppy

Rafael had read Proverbs 26:11 several times, but he had never fully understood it, until he bought a dog he named Jack. With great affection, he gave food to his doggie, played with him, took care of his bathing, combed his hair, and even took him to the vet every now and then.

One day, as Rafael got delayed in some errands before coming home, the pup got desperately hungry. As his food bowl was already empty, it seems like he went out to the backyard and ate something that wasn't very healthy. As he came back home, Jack's owner realized the doggie had vomited. Hungry as he was, Rafael went to the kitchen in order to warm up some food and came back right away to pick up the disgusting mess. To his horror, as the man walked towards the backyard he noted Jack was eating his own vomit. The puppy had to endure three or four heavy scoldings while Rafael picked up the vomit.

The Bible says that "as a dog returns to its vomit, so fools repeat their folly" (Prov. 26:11). The attitude of some of us could be compared, at least in part, with Jack's gross act. God has called us out of darkness into His wonderful light and, nevertheless, we fall into sin again and again as if we did not appreciate being by God's side.

In his second epistle, Apostle Peter warns against this danger. According to him, even after we have "escaped the corruption of the world by knowing our Lord and Savior Jesus Christ," we run the risk of getting entangled again in the same things and end up worse than before (2 Pet. 2:20). Although it may seem cruel, when Peter describes people who suffer this kind of backsliding he compares them with a dog who returns to its own vomit, and also compares them with a pig that, after being washed, goes back to roll in the mud (v. 22)

**Is life like a rocking chair?**

Sadly, relapsing into sin is much more common than what most people can notice at first glance. We all suffer from that problem, even if we find it hard to acknowledge it.

Has it ever happened to you as with Paul, who confessed that although he wanted to do good, sometimes he found himself doing wrong? The Apostle once wrote, "So I find this law at work: Although I want to do good, evil is right there with me. For in my inner being I delight in God's law; but I see another law at work in me, waging war against the law of my mind and making me a prisoner of the law of sin at work within me" (Rom. 7:21-23).

Indeed, life is like a rocking chair. And our decisions, our businesses, and even the church often rock back and forth on it. Throughout my years in pastoral ministry, I have seen this problem repeatedly in the lives of too many people, and I have suffered it myself. Is it really impossible to escape the "rocking chair" of human nature which oscillates between good and evil, success and failure, happiness and sadness, repentance and sin? Are we trapped in a rocking chair?

> Indeed, life is like a rocking chair. And our decisions, our businesses, and even the church often rock back and forth on it.

In the Garden of Gethsemane, Jesus Himself faced the tremendous problem of life's rocking chair. In the hour when He most desperately needed his friends by his side, He asked them to go with Him to the garden to pray. The One who had always been source of comfort and encouragement for the disciples now called them, confided that he was "overwhelmed with sorrow to the point of death" (Matt. 26:38), and asked for their support and prayer. After praying and agonizing by Himself, Jesus went back to them thirsty of His friends' company. The troubled Savior hoped to hear from them some words that would help Him bear the heavy burden. But "their eyes were heavy. They did not know what to say to him" (Mark 14:40). Again and again, Jesus came back to His disciples seeking their support, only to find them asleep.

Jesus Himself was subject to the pressures of human nature's "rocking chair." He deeply felt the need to save humankind. But the burden was so heavy that, in His humanity, He begged the Father three times to take that painful cup away from Him. In that moment, "the destiny of a lost world trembled in the balance. Should He refuse to drink the cup, the result would be eternal ruin to the human race."[2]

But Jesus was victorious in His struggle that night in Gethsemane, and He reaffirmed His decision to redeem us, even as He had to pay the highest price. A few years later, when Paul struggled with his temptations and felt miserable because of his desperate oscillation between sin and godliness, he found in Jesus the solution to his own crisis.

Many Christians, including myself in the first place, could cry out like Paul, in desperation: "What a wretched man I am! Who will rescue me from this body that is subject to death?" But we have no reason to give up. Paul's desperate cry is followed by a wonderful exclamation of hope. Right after asking "Who will rescue me?" he provided the answer: "Thanks be to God, who delivers me through Jesus Christ our Lord!" (Rom. 7:24, 25).

Everybody at church thought Bernie was a really good Christian. But he knew it was different. It all started when he was 9 years old and innocently stumbled across a crumpled-up page of a porn magazine, but that encounter was the seed for masturbation and a life of struggles with lust. Yes, he knew he was doing wrong, and he really wanted to get away from porn. He confessed and repented of his sin daily, but only to give in to temptation a week or so later.[3] Bernie struggled with pornography as a boy, a young man, and, ultimately, as a pastor. His life showed a predictable pattern of temptation, failure, guilt and shame, recommitment, and back to failure, only to start the cycle again.

Several years later, after God's mighty hand delivered Bernie from porn, he wrote a book where he boldly told his story and the way

God freed him. One of the things that hit me was his statement that "in my ministry as a pastor I've found that the most common spiritual struggle—especially for men, regardless of age or background—is in the area of sexual sin."[4] We all struggle in life's rocking chairs.

Plenty of images come to my mind: A newly-baptized Adventist who cries out for help regarding his old urges for smoking and drinking; a good-looking lady who is unable to find her way out of marijuana and prostitution although she has been caught by the police several times; a respected church elder who confessed to me he had been hiding a forbidden sexual relationship with a female church member; a young preacher with great skills who just can't get away from his three secret sex pals. Although all of this may seem to be just too much, if you analyze your life you'll probably find that you're struggling in life's rocking chair as well. Is there any way out?

When Jesus announced that all His disciples would be ashamed of Him, Peter thought it was just absurd to disown his Master, so he promised that even if everybody else would run away from Jesus, he would still be faithful. The caring Master, who knows how weak we human beings are, kindly warned Peter that he would deny Jesus three times that very night. Jesus's words were almost drowned by Peter's quick and sincere answer, "Even if I have to die with you, I will never disown you" (Matt. 26:35). But that night's experience would teach Peter that he was unable to win in his struggle with sin without Jesus's help. Just as the Savior had announced, Peter denied Jesus three times that night.

When the impulsive Peter heard the second crowing of the cock, he was still speaking nasty words in another futile attempt to

hide from others his affiliation with Jesus. It was right at that moment when the Savior turned His eyes away from the insulting judges and with the deepest love looked upon His wretched disciple who was suffering in the rocking chair of temptation as he disowned Jesus again and again. At the same time, Peter's eyes were attracted to his Master, and Jesus's compassionate and forgiving look pierced Peter's heart like an arrow.[5]

That's right. We are talking about Peter, the apostle who said those who meet the Lord and fall back into sin are like a dog that goes back to its vomit and like a pig that after being washed goes back to roll in the mud. Peter did not escape the pressures of life's rocking chair either.

But far from being a source of discouragement, Peter's example ends up being very encouraging for us. The person who disowned Jesus three times in the court had to weep bitterly that night, but he also came to love Jesus very deeply, and he became one of the most powerful heralds of the gospel in his days. In one of his sermons, Peter made an altar call and some three thousand people accepted the challenge and were baptized (Acts 2:41). My point here is that, just like Peter, by God's grace we can be successful too.

## Memories of my childhood

The motor of that old ramshackle little taxi was roaring frightfully, perhaps complaining about the lots of weight it was bearing up that hill. My mom has always been one of those women who don't know how to travel lightly. She packs more than you would imagine, just in case someone in the family needs anything else (perhaps she's right, though). She was in the front seat with five or six bags by her feet plus a suitcase on her lap. My dad was riding by the rear left window, also overloaded. Although I was being uncomfortably sandwiched between my brother and my sister, I reached out through the rear right window and I was able to see grandpa's gray-haired head. Unforgettable!

When the car finally made it to our destination at the top of that little hill, my grandpa's rocking chair was still swinging him back and forth and making that typical sound, both squeaky and pleasant at the same time. My grandpa loved his rocking chair, and I must admit I did too.

During my childhood, my parents moved several times from one town to the other. But, regardless of the place where we would be living, we traveled every year to my grandparents' home. That was our most likely vacation spot. There were no exquisite beaches or fancy hotels, but my grandparents were there, and also the kids in the neighborhood who already knew we were coming and were expectant to play with us all day. Grandpa Ben's rocking chair was also there, of course.

I have seen rocking chairs in different colors, styles, and materials. Some rocking chairs, especially targeted at children, are shaped like little horses. Others are designed for moms to rock their babies. Some are hanging rocking chairs, while others stand on the floor. There's one-seat, multiple-seat, and even bed-type rocking chairs. One day a particular rocking chair caught my attention because it had three seats, one in the middle for dad or grandpa, and the other two on both sides for children to sit and listen to stories or just enjoy the rocking.

Grandpa Ben died several years ago, and I have no idea where his dearly-cherished rocking chair is anymore. But another rocking chair, much bigger than my grandpa's, has been catching my eye lately. It's not made of wood, or plastic, or metal. It is made up of seconds, minutes, hours, and days, combined with the breath of life God originally breathed into Adam. Human beings seem to be sitting in that rocking chair from the day they are born until they die. It is the rocking chair of life.

Life's oscillations are not limited to matters of spiritual nature. It is possible to see certain repetitive patterns in almost every aspect of human life. And such movements respond to certain laws. Throughout the next few chapters, we will explore together the principles behind every swing in the rocking chair of life.

**THINK-IT-THROUGH AND APPLICATION QUESTIONS**

1. In which ways do you think Jack's attitude is similar to ours when we go back to sin?

...................................................................................

...................................................................................

...................................................................................

2. Why do you think Peter was unable to keep his promise?

...................................................................................

...................................................................................

...................................................................................

3. Can you think of some ways in which you have recently failed God? Do you think it's worth asking God for His forgiveness and help?

...................................................................................

...................................................................................

...................................................................................

# References for this chapter

[1]M. J. Ryan. *This year I will. . .: How to finally change a habit, keep a resolution, or make a dream come true.* New York, NY: Broadway Books, 2006, p. 2.

[2]Ellen White. *Testimony Treasures,* volume 3, p. 337.

[3]Bernie Anderson. *Breaking the Silence: A pastor goes public about his battle with pornography.* 2007. Silver Spring, MD: AutumnHouse, pp. 24, 25.

[4]Ibid., 11.

[5]Ellen White. *The Desire of Ages,* pp. 712-713.

# THE ROCKING CHAIR OF LIFE

S OME of the young folks who were playing in the basketball court noticed William looked a little more exhausted than usual. He would score a goal every now and then, but he was constantly huffing and puffing. Although he was no longer a teenager like the other guys, the exhaustion he felt this time seemed so strange to William that he decided to sit down under the shade of a tree by the right side of the court. But the feeling of tiredness, excessive sweating and shortness of breath still persisted some fifteen minutes later, and his wife Sandra noticed William's face was a little pale.

—Take me to the hospital, honey.

Many hospitals are famous for their long waiting times, but that particular day a nurse noticed something strange in William and measured his vital signs right away. Suddenly, the patient and his wife saw themselves surrounded by physicians and nurses checking different things each. After a seemingly endless night and more tests in the morning, a physician came to tell William he had suffered a heart attack: One of his veins was completely clogged, and another one was 75 percent obstructed.

The astonished couple could barely believe what their ears had heard. How in the world had all that happened?

It all started one August morning several years ago, or at least that was what William was able to recall. Right after taking his shower that day, he came up with the idea of getting on the scale his wife used to watch her weight every day. William got scared with what he saw. When he realized how much weight he had gained, he promised to himself he would start a diet on that very day. And so he did, as a good man of his word. Although he lost 20 pounds during the diet, the season of family birthdays and holiday meals came right afterwards, so every single pound came back.

Next summer William started another diet and his weight went down, but things did not go as he had planned, and by January our friend had gained all that weight again, and some more. The cycle repeated itself year after year and, without William realizing it, his veins started pooling fat and slowly clogging themselves, until that strange afternoon in the basketball court.

**The rocking chair of diets and hunger**

Sadly, William is not the only one who has experienced problems with weight oscillation. Billions of dollars are spent every year in weight-loss products and services, but apparently the greatest challenge is not in losing weight but in maintaining weight loss. Reduction in calorie intake (which is characteristic of diets) seems to lead to a feeling of hunger that ends up in people returning to old habits and finally the dreaded weight gain. In fact, it is estimated that at least 80 percent of those who slim down after a diet gain some or all of the weight back within one year.[1]

To make things worse, several recent studies suggest that a shortage of willpower might not be the only reason for people backsliding into old bad eating habits and the return to those extra pounds. According to current research, this is what might be happening: when you lose weight certain hormones like leptin will start waging war against your intentions to lose weight. They will make you feel much hungrier and will also cause your calories to burn more slowly. This is the "perfect storm" for weight regain![2]

Simply put, your hormones might be guilty, at least in part, for your weight regain after a diet. Millions of people have realized with disappointment that their intentions to lose weight seem to be condemned to failure: Hunger leads to eating, and eating leads to gaining weight, which leads to dieting, but this leads to hunger, and the cycle repeats itself apparently with no definite solution.

## Other types of rocking chairs in life

Cristy, a 34-year-old woman who has smoked since she was 19, quit smoking in 2001 by using patches. She stayed smoke-free for 2 years, but in the process gained 20 pounds and got depressed, which caused her to backslide into smoking. In 2005 she sought medical help and was able to stop smoking again by using pills, but when she stopped taking medications the craving for cigarettes became uncontrollable again. In 2009, desperate, she made her third attempt at quitting and published her story in a women's forum on the Web with the intention of seeking help and partners in her struggle. Sad to say, too many people around the world suffer just like Cristy in what seems to be an endless oscillating pattern. Is there any way out?

Michael was raised a Christian, and he sincerely loves God. But he has not been able to overcome his homosexual desires. Like Paul prayed about something else and called it a "thorn in my flesh" (2 Cor. 12:7), Michael has prayed fervently, even desperately, for God to take away those unwanted same-sex urges. He firmly believes that homosexuality was not in God's original creative plan for humanity. He openly says that homosexuality is rather a tragic sign that human nature and relationships have been broken by sin and that therefore homosexual practice goes against God's express will for human beings. But he's found out that there's a tough, long way to go from saying it to doing it. He has experienced stinging rejection from fellow Christians almost every time he's tried to come out of the closet and ask for prayer. He even married Carla, a beautiful, young woman, sincerely hoping that it would help, but nothing changed. Is Michael condemned to this struggle? Does God have any hope for him?

Mary cries a lot. Her husband John, a certified public accountant, makes a great deal of money through his permanent contracts with various public and private organizations. But all the money he makes has not been able to solve his problem of alcohol addiction and all that it comes with. A few years ago, they started attending church and he quit drinking. Some time went by. I recall it as if it was yesterday when I baptized them. He was eventually elected to be a deacon, and she was appointed women's ministries leader in

their church. Mary still sticks to her faith, but John has backslid into drinking countless times. Every time he relapses, he becomes violent with her. Although he asks her for forgiveness and intends to quit drinking, he fails again. Just like him, millions of people in the world are staggering from drinking to sobriety and then back to drinking, in another seemingly endless cycle.

The list of issues keeps going. A study in the United States revealed that almost half of those who were released from prison in 2004 were reincarcerated within three years because of some other offense or because they violated some of the conditions of their release.[3] Common sense suggests that if someone is found driving drunk and suffers some consequence they should stop such misconduct. For this reason, the elevated rates of recidivism in driving under the influence of alcohol are a significant source of concern. On the other hand, thousands of people get trapped between the irregular cycles of the stock market. They make lots of money in one particular day, only to lose all of it sometime next week or next month in another horrible cycle that has led many to bankruptcy.

I wish oscillations between success and failure were limited to the stock market, smoking, alcoholism, diets, criminal recidivism, sexual behavior and drunk driving. But the unfortunate truth is that this problem seems to affect almost all aspects of life.

It could be said that even our planet seems to experience this phenomenon. The earth rotates around its own axis every 24 hours, so the light of days and the darkness of nights alternate in consecutive cycles while human beings can do nothing to change that. The movement of the earth around the sun, which takes some 365 days, causes relatively cyclical changes in seasons (spring, summer, autumn and winter), and marks the duration of an entire year. Again, the patterns are repetitive.

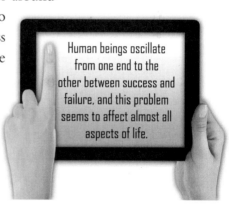

Human beings oscillate from one end to the other between success and failure, and this problem seems to affect almost all aspects of life.

Since the nineteenth century, some physicians started recording and analyzing the human body's biorhythms, in what they perceived as repetitive cycles in a number of diseases. There are those who believe human beings are condemned to oscillate in repetitive patterns in almost all areas of life. It is said that biorhythms follow a regular wave, oscillating back and forth over the length of the cycle. Although there is not enough scientific evidence for all that is said regarding biorhythms, some of these cycles in human beings are generally recognized by most people. Examples include the sleep cycle and women's menstrual cycle, among others.[4] Are we really trapped between repetitive cycles in life?

## Beyond the rocking chair

It's very early, before the crack of dawn, and I wake up on my tiptoes, a little worried. My wife Natalia is on our bed, sound asleep. I walk by the room where Ángel, my little boy, is lying on his side on the edge of his bed. When I get to the room that belongs to Natasha, my youngest daughter, I realize she completely took off her blanket. She's so profoundly asleep that she is not even sucking her finger.

Now I'm sitting in my home's little office, in front of my laptop. I drink a huge glass of water. I'm thinking about the human tragedy, and also about my own personal struggles.

I close my eyes and ask God why: It seems incredible to me that this life is so painful and unstable. The experiences of John, William, Michael and Cristy represent the lives of millions of people in the world who seem to be simply oscillating between success and failure. Not even the church escapes this issue. We seem to be swinging without any reason from one extreme of our needs or desires to the other, as if we were here with no purpose at all. I pray that God will open my eyes every day that I might see beyond the rocking chair.

**THINK-IT-THROUGH AND APPLICATION QUESTIONS**

1. What do the experiences of William, Michael, Cristy, and John have in common?

...................................................................................................

...................................................................................................

...................................................................................................

...................................................................................................

2. Can you recall a situation in which you have felt like in a "rocking chair," oscillating from success to failure and back again? What would you ask God about that?

...................................................................................................

...................................................................................................

...................................................................................................

...................................................................................................

# References for this chapter

[1]Amanda MacMillan. After dieting, hormone changes may fuel weight regain http://www.cnn.com/2011/10/26/health/post-diet-weight-regain

[2]Rudolph Leibel y Michael Rosenbaum. Metabolic responses to weight perturbation. In K. Clément, B.M. Spiegelman, and Y. Christen, eds. *Novel Insights into Adipose Cell Functions,* p. 121-134. New York, NY: Springer, 2010.

[3]The Pew Center on the States. State of Recidivism: *The Revolving Door of America's Prisons* (Washington, DC: The Pew Charitable Trusts, Abril 2011), p.2.

[4]Fatik Baran Mandal. *Textbook of Animal Behaviour.* New Delhi, India: PHI, 2010, p. 248.

THERE'S still a long time before this airplane gets to its destination, so I decided to write a little bit right here. I open the cover of the window on my right side, getting closer in order to get a better view. The sky looks clear and beautiful in its upper part, but I can see under the airplane several heavy clouds that look like cotton pellets, some bigger than others.

My seat is just in front of one the airplane's wings. I look back through the window in order to better appreciate the shape of the wing. Though I've been flying for years, I'm always amazed at how such a heavy structure can fly so high and so fast. I have to admit that although nearly 65 million passengers traveled by airplane in the United States last thirty days and countless others worldwide (several of them were even sitting in a spot like this),[1] many of them did not even think about the structure which took them from one place to the other. Even so, I still cannot get over my amazement.

Most people don't even wonder what the distance between the tips of the two big wings might be. Yet those who designed the aircraft carefully calculated every tiny detail in them, bearing in mind that whether the airplane is going to be able to fly or not largely depends upon those wings. There are also two rear, horizontal wings which are very tiny if compared with their impressive front counterparts. Without these tiny wings, however, the aircraft would be much more likely to swing up and down out of control. The rear vertical wing, also largely unnoticed, is responsible for keeping the aircraft from suddenly yawing left or right.

We could keep talking about the function of every single part of the airplane, but that's not the point. The most meaningful thing right now is the importance of structure in the process of causing an airplane to fly. The relationship between the different parts of the aircraft is aimed at a successful flight from liftoff to landing. Such a relationship is known as structure.

How can I apply this to my life? I open my Bible and read: "It is God who arms me with strength and keeps my way secure. He makes my feet like the feet of a deer; he causes me to stand on the heights." (Ps. 18:32, 33). I think of William's struggles with his extra pounds, and I ponder Cristy's fight against the habit of smoking. Then I take a moment to pray for John, who has not yet been able to overcome his alcohol craving, and I also pray for Elizabeth and Michael, who tumble between faithfulness to God and their own weaknesses. It seems very sad to me that people with such good intentions experience so many failures.

Apostle Paul invites us to "hold unswervingly to the hope we profess, for he who promised is faithful" (Heb. 10:23). The small rear horizontal wings and the vertical one, which work as stabilizers in an airplane, come to my mind again. If an airplane as big as the one I am currently in is able to fly, it is encouraging for me to think that God is able to make it possible for William, Cristy, Elizabeth, you and I to fly over our problems and succeed as well. But how?

The safest way to fly above our problems and succeed is by doing it through a structure that is designed to achieve it. Maybe there will be difficulties, and obstacles of various sorts may come. Maybe the results we get will not be completely perfect all the time, but if every single decision we make is oriented towards "flying the plane," we will make it to our destination.

On July 8, 2010, an airplane piloted by André Borschberg made history by flying during 26 hours without using gas at all. Not satisfied with such achievement, Borschberg, Bertrand Piccard and the rest of their team set out to do a series of flights that would cross the USA from the East to the West coast without using a single drop of fuel. And they were able to achieve it, on July 6, 2013. How did they get it done? The structure of Borschberg and Piccard's plane is designed to work with solar energy alone, and it can even store energy to be used during the night.[2]

OK, I agree. Structure is not all that is needed to cause a plane to fly. You may have an airplane with the perfect structure, but if the aircraft doesn't have some kind of fuel or energy source, it probably won't fly. Regardless of how carefully the plane's design has been calculated, a pilot or some other control system is necessary for the aircraft to fly (well, you could argue that fuel and pilot are also a part of structure, but that's another story). My point is that even though structure is not all an airplane needs in order to fly, you still have to consider structure. Otherwise, the plane won't fly anyway.

It would be dangerously crazy to start flying an airplane whose structure is damaged, even if the pilot is an expert. Another similar folly would be to fly an aircraft without knowing its structure, ignoring which buttons or levers to push or pull in order to manoeuver the plane. If someone jumps on a motorcycle in an airport's take-off runway and speeds up as much as they can —hoping the bike will climb up to the 3600 feet (10,9 Km) some planes get to—we'd probably think such person went  crazy. A motorcycle's structure is not good for flying, but airplanes were designed to achieve a successfulliftoff, flight and landing, taking people and their stuff safely fromone place to the other.

That's why it is important to know concepts related to structure. Most people "fly" throughout life without asking how everything works, but that doesn't mean knowing it is not important. Knowing the structure of life's "rocking chair" will definitely help us understand why we oscillate in such a predictable way between success and failure, and it could help us fly more steadily towards our greatest dreams.

**Towards a definition of structure**

As important as understanding matters related to structure might be, it's not an easy task. To begin with, consistent and scientific analyses of structure are very recent. And to complicate things even more, the concept of structure in a certain culture will probably not be the same in another culture.

Now, "structure" can be defined as the relationships among the parts of an organized whole. Bridges and buildings, the human body and flowers, computers, family and society, even this book you're reading and the relationship that exists between one paragraph and the next—all those things are structures.[3]

This brings us to the issue of mission. The key question in order to understand the concept of mission is, "What were things designed for?" The structure of a bridge is designed for people or vehicles to cross over them from one side to the other. Chairs are designed to hold those who decide to sit on them. Rocking chairs were made so we can rock in then. Cars were designed to transport people or things from one place to the other, by land. Airplanes were made to fly. We were made to glorify God and to live forever with Him.

The term "mission" refers to the purpose for which things, people, and organizations—including the church—exist. Richard Daft puts it this way: "All organizations, including MySpace, Johnson & Johnson, Google, Harvard University, the Catholic Church [and all other denominations, including the Seventh-day Adventist Church], the U.S. Department of Agriculture, the local laundry, and the neighborhood deli, exist for a purpose. This purpose may be referred to as the overall goal, or mission."[4]

**Why do rocking chairs oscillate?**

Good question. The simplest answer is that rocking chairs oscillate because they were made for that purpose. A more elaborate answer would have to explain the structure of the rocking chair and its natural tendency to oscillate.

People and organizations alike have moments of success, and some of such moments are unforgettable. But too often moments of "success" are followed by a decline or failure, as if it were just normal that failure comes after success. A fabulous first day of working out seems to predict a very healthy summer, but then two or three days (or maybe an entire month) of inactivity will come next, and we forget what we promised. In an exciting moment of communion with God, we feel His presence and promise we'll fully give ourselves to Him every single day. As hard as it might be to explain it, however, we realize just a little later that there's no time to pray, to read the Bible, or to talk to others about God's love. A month of dramatic business success seems to predict the best year of the company, but next month sales are so down that the manager goes crazy trying to understand why. Sounds familiar?

In the context of organizations, it is said that the duration of success largely depends upon structure. An organization is either structured to advance constantly or to oscillate between success and failure. Any type of action occurring in an organization structured to advance has an entirely different effect than it would in an organization structured to oscillate. Success "succeeds" in organizations structured to advance, but it is neutralized in organizations that are structured to oscillate.[5]

In a similar way, oscillations in life–those desperate cycles of losing and gaining weight, stopping the habit of smoking and backsliding on it again and again, asking God for His forgiveness regarding a particular sin only to fall back several times right there— do have an explanation. Simply put, structure could bear much of the blame, and changing the structure might be the best solution. Robert Fritz explains this by saying that "if we found ourselves in a rocking chair, but we wanted to travel downtown, we would not attempt to 'fix' our rocking chair by putting wheels on it, or by installing a motor, steering wheel, and brakes. We would move from the rocking chair to a car."[6]

Swinging back and forth can be very enjoyable in a rocking chair, but in the world of organizations oscillating is not the nicest thing. Sadly, however, most organizations have many oscillating patterns.

Success in the company generally leads to expansion, but then financial pressures lead to cost-cutting and personnel downsizing, only to again face the need for expansion and investment very soon. Decision-making can go from centralization to decentralization and then recentralization when things go wrong, in another rocking chair pattern. Long-term plans generally end up being sidelined because of emergencies, but then long-term realities call the managers' attention once again, and the cycle tends to repeat itself time and time again. In the meantime, the organization squanders money, time, and many other resources.[7] That is also true in people's real lives!

### Why do organizations oscillate?

The basic unit of structure is the tension-resolution system. Once a tension exists, it generates a tendency to move towards resolving such tension. When you feel very thirsty, it's usually because your body has less water than it needs, therefore such tension creates in you a desire to look for water or some liquid to drink. When the amount of liquid you drink is similar to the one your body needs, your normal reaction would be to stop fluid intake.[8] Very few people millimetrically calculate the amount of water they will drink or have specific mandatory moments in their schedule in order to drink water or stop drinking it. The process generally occurs naturally.

> Organizations oscillate because of one simple reason: their structure is not well aligned with mission. And that's just why people oscillate as well!

The same thing happens in organizations. When an administrator's main concern is the intensity of problems, he or she will always be busy. When a problem comes up, it will call the administration's attention until it is solved. Administrative actions apparently produced a good effect, because they reduced the intensity of the problem that seemed to be causing trouble. Since now "everything is ok," administrative action ceases, and that causes the problem to eventually come back. And then another problem will emerge, and yet another one, causing managers to spend their time always busy solving problems. The net result is oscillation. Companies and managers end up being always busy, but going nowhere.

Organizations oscillate because of one simple reason: their structure is not well aligned with mission. And that's just why people oscillate as well! If people, organizations or even the church want to experience true success, they need to fix their structure, aligning it with mission. If structure is defined as the relationship among the elements of a whole, and mission is the *raison d'être* of structure, then the solution is in making sure everything we do as individuals, organizations, or churches is aligned with mission. Next chapter explains how to make that happen.

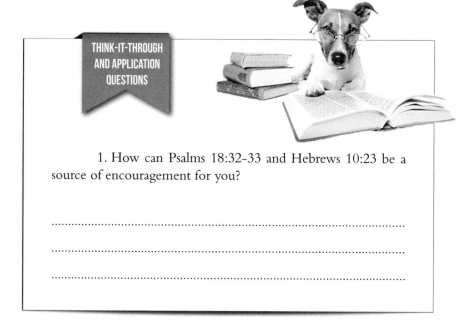

**THINK-IT-THROUGH AND APPLICATION QUESTIONS**

1. How can Psalms 18:32-33 and Hebrews 10:23 be a source of encouragement for you?

.................................................................................

.................................................................................

.................................................................................

2. This chapter insists that "organizations oscillate because of one simple reason: their structure is not well aligned with mission. And that's just why people oscillate as well!" What do you think you can do to avoid oscillating between success and failure?

...................................................................................................................

...................................................................................................................

...................................................................................................................

## References for this chapter

[1] U.S. Department of Transportation. BTS Data. Available at http://www.rita.dot.gov/bts/sites/rita.dot.gov.bts/files/bts28_13_0.pdf

[2] See both reports at http://www.solarimpulse.com/timeline/view/6713; http://www.solarimpulse.com/en/across-america/new-york-city/).

[3] Hatch, *Organization Theory,* 161; Pullan y Bhadeshia, eds., *Structure in Science and Art, 1.*

[4] Richard L. Daft, *Organization Theory and Design* (Mason, OH: South-Western Cengage Learning, 2010), 60.

[5] See Robert Fritz, *Corporate Tides: The Inescapable Laws of Organizational Structure* (San Francisco, CA: Berrett-Koehler Publishers, 1996) 11, 12.

[6] Ibid., 44, 45.

[7] Ibid., 33, 36.

[8] Ibid., 18-22.

## WHY DO ROCKING CHAIRS OSCILLATE?
### PART 2

J ESSICA is a business manager. She knows by heart her organization's mission statement, which is hanging on a nice frame in her office and it's just what her employees and customers see as soon as they get in there. However, Jessica cannot understand why her company doesn't have long-lasting success. She is also a Christian, and knows Matthew 28:18-20 by heart; yet she's been struggling with secret temptations for longer than she can recall.

According to Fritz, since the basic unit of structure is the tension-resolution system, the key to stop oscillation is to establish a structural tension that will tend to resolve in the direction of the organization's mission. Such statement may seem too simplistic at first glance, but it's loaded with meaning. If a manager wants their organization to stop oscillating and wants it to start moving towards permanent success instead, he or she needs to focus their organization on mission. But there's such a huge distance from saying to doing! This chapter is an introduction to how to achieve it in organizations, in the church, and in our personal lives.

Jessica's concern makes sense. Defining mission (the desired results) might qualify as the most fundamental—and perhaps most difficult—decision a nonprofit has to make, and this decision is often a heavy burden for top administrators.[1] But the work is not done when we define mission. Organizations need much more than a mission statement hanging in a wall on the manager's office. When evaluating the organization's structure, administrators need to evaluate whether it facilitates or hinders the fulfillment of mission.[2]

From this perspective, if an organization's leaders want to experience long-lasting success, aligning all the organization's decisions with the fulfillment of mission is not merely a good idea but an obligation. Henry Mintzberg maintains that the "strategic apex," where he says you can find "those people charged with overall responsibility for the organization—the chief executive officer (whether called president, superintendent, Pope, or whatever), and any other top-level managers whose concerns are global," must ensure that the organization serves its mission in an effective way.[3]

### So what?

A long discussion on the administrative implications of a mission statement might be enjoyable for a person who earns their living in business administration—well, I won't guarantee, but perhaps it will—yet it is not necessarily the most exciting thing for the rest of us. So in the middle of this discussion I decided to pause for a moment and ask a very important question right here. What is this good for in real life? Let me put it this way:

Many organizations attempt to build a philosophical platform of action by the creation of a mission statement, a vision statement, and a set of values. But such statements are rarely seen as the guiding force that determines the major decisions. Fritz suggests that instead of relying on slogans, managers could communicate the organization's mission by managerial actions, decisions, strategies, and policies that are consistent with the mission, because "actions do speak louder than words."[4]

When Jesus tried to teach this very lesson in another context, the Bible says some who heard him were amazed. I love the way Jesus explained it:

> Therefore everyone who hears these words of mine and puts them into practice is like a wise man who built his house on the rock. The rain came down, the streams rose, and the winds blew and beat against that house; yet it did not fall, because it had its foundation on the rock. But everyone who hears these words of

mine and does not put them into practice is like a foolish man who built his house on sand. The rain came down, the streams rose, and the winds blew and beat against that house, and it fell with a great crash (Matthew 7:24-27).

It's not the mission statement what will change the life of the organization, nor the theoretical acceptance of God's Word what will save the sinner. As an apostle said, "as the body without the spirit is dead, so faith without deeds is dead" (James 2:26).

## Mission as the guiding force

When there is no guiding force for each and every one of the administrative decisions in an organization, it is impossible to predict where the organization might be heading in the long run. The only thing that can be anticipated is that it will not experience long-lasting success. Similarly, when a person's life does not have a guiding force for all their decisions, the only thing we can know in advance is that he or she is not going to reach the heights God wants human beings to reach.

Employees pull organizations in different directions, depending upon their role in the company and other factors. Consequently, unless measures are taken so that mission governs all decisions, it will be virtually impossible to reach agreements on important matters, and the organization will end up oscillating.

People at the "strategic apex" (those at the top of the organization) exert centralizing pressures through command-and-control management and rules. Those at the operating core (the people directly related to the production of services or products seek to control their own destiny and minimize influence from ot' structural components. Middle managers pull the organization toward "silo management" (departments tend to operate independently and information fails to flow easily throughout the company). People at the "techno-structure" level (the analysts who design, plan, change, or train the operating core) exert pressure to standardize in order to monitor and measure. The support staff's pull is toward authority being given to small work units so that there is more collaboration and so that they can have influence over daily decision-making.

This concept has logical implications in the context of a worldwide organization such as the Seventh-day Adventist Church. Unless intentional measures are taken so that the church's mission (to make disciples among all ethnic groups) dominates all the decisions at all levels of the organization, the same kind of pressures just described will emerge.

And that's just what is happening, in many ways. The initiatives coming from the "strategic apex" (the General Conference) usually tend to lead the world church in a direction that, although very good, is very different from the one many in the "operating core" (pastors and local leaders) would prefer. Middle managers (administrators at the Conference or Union level and in a sense even at the Division level) tend to handle their field with a vision that is limited to their own area, often forgetting the church's mission in other parts of the world.

The net result is that, with so much pressure from so many different places, the church wobbles from one place to the other without being able to advance. Perhaps without realizing it, the church might end up ignoring its mission of reaching the unreached. After all, the unreached have no representation in the boards where decisions are made at the different administrative levels of the church. It could easily happen that there's nobody that pulls the church towards intentional efforts directed to reaching the unreached with the gospel.

## Measuring success in terms of mission

Organizational success can be defined as "strong management and sound governance that enables an organization to move steadily toward its goals, to adapt to change, and to innovate." From this perspective, effectiveness is better evaluated in the light of the

**SUCCESS MUST BE EVALUATED
IN TERMS OF MISSION**

organization's mission, by comparing the service provided with the agency's objectives. However, "most nonprofit groups track their performance by metrics such as dollars raised, membership growth, number of visitors, people served, and overhead costs."[5]

As important as these metrics might be, they do not measure the real success of an organization in achieving its mission. An institution may find itself surviving economically or even having some sort of "success" but not making any significant progress towards achieving its mission. When there is no intentionality in an organization for creating employee performance metrics that are aligned with mission, somebody will create some sort of measure to evaluate or report performance, even if such measures do not really say anything about success in mission. Then, if numbers look good, leaders feel everything is perfectly fine, even though the organization is not really achieving its mission.

Success should be evaluated in terms of mission. Just imagine a rocking chair that doesn't rock, a car that doesn't drive, a beautifully-designed aircraft that (unfortunately) doesn't fly, or a bridge that can't bridge the two points it's supposed to span. An organization that doesn't fulfill its mission has become worthless, and a human being who doesn't live by his or her God-given purpose has overlooked the most important thing in life.

Measuring success in the achievement of mission is arguably the most difficult of the assessment tasks an organization might have to do, but it is also the most important one, because it has to do with the organization's raison d'être. Likewise, the most important thing we human beings must evaluate is whether or not we are fulfilling the mission God created us for.

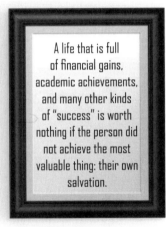

A life that is full of financial gains, academic achievements, and many other kinds of "success" is worth nothing if the person did not achieve the most valuable thing: their own salvation.

It is perfectly possible—and pretty scary—for a person to spend their entire life running after different goals, only to realize at the end of it all that nothing really worthwhile was achieved. A life that is full of financial gains, academic achievements, and many other kinds of "success" is worth nothing if the person did not achieve the most valuable thing: their own salvation. Jesus Himself explained it through this rhetorical question: "What good is it for someone to gain the whole world, yet forfeit their soul?" (Mark 8:36).

Although the idea that it's necessary to measure success in terms of mission may be "simple, even obvious," very few people actually apply it intentionally and constantly. Furthermore, very few nonprofits have systematically linked their performance metrics to mission, and too many institutions repeat the mistake of confusing institutional achievements with progress toward achieving mission.[6]

## Mission versus goals

It all started in the afternoon of Thursday, August 10, 1978. At 5:45 p.m., Judy left home very happy, driving her 1973 yellow Ford Pinto. Her sister Lynn and her cousin Donna were also riding with her. The three girls were heading to Goshen First Baptist Church, for a volleyball practice. Due to some unknown problem, the girls decided to turn around and Judy turned on the emergency flashers. Her car was travelling at no more than 20 miles per hour when another car suddenly hit them from behind. A few seconds later, their Ford Pinto was engulfed in flames. Two of the girls died on the scene, and Judy died later in the hospital. Ford Motor Company was accused in the three girls' death.[7] Why would the company who built the cars be accused on the death of these girls?

At the end of the 1960s, the Ford Company seemed to be under threat by other car makers who were selling small, fuel-efficient models. As a desperate intent of making headway against its competitors, Ford announced a new car design that would be less than 2000 pounds, would cost under 2000 dollars, and would be available in a few months. In their hurry to fulfill the goal, the company omitted some safety checks, and did not correct a problem that would prove fatal: the new Ford Pinto was very likely to ignite upon rear impact, even at low speeds. In a study presented at Harvard University, Lisa Ordóñez and her associate researchers indicate that "after Ford finally discovered the hazard, executives remained committed to their goal and instead of repairing the faulty design, calculated that the costs of lawsuits associated with Pinto fires (which involved 53 deaths and many injuries) would be less than the cost of fixing the design."[8]

Although after many hours of deliberation the jury finally found Ford not guilty of the manslaughter charges, this incident illustrates how dangerous goals can be when they are not properly administered. And, sad to say, there is a big difference between mission and the goals that often guide organizations, churches, and people.

Very often, people and companies evaluate their "success" with measurements that really don't say anything about true success. Too often, goals that have nothing to do with mission are given extreme attention, and keep people and companies oscillating between success and failure.

An extreme example of goal idolatry is the 1996 Mount Everest disaster. Rob Hall and Scott Fischer had successfully guided climbers several times up and down that mountain. Many people usually paid huge amounts of money so these veterans would lead them through the adventure. But on that day, a combination of bad weather and poor decisions caused the death of eight people on the way down—including the two experienced climbers. Hall and Fischer apparently succumbed to the pressure of competition with each other, decided to get to the top in spite of the weather, and it all ended up in tragedy.

The book Destructive Goal Pursuit is inspired in the events of that disaster and its implications for leadership. In an analysis of that work, Becky de Oliveira suggests the events related to the Everest disaster "have very real implications for anyone in leadership—particularly in Christian leadership, where we need to achieve 'goals'—such as conversions or baptisms."[9]

Towards the end of her analysis, the author directs her readers' attention to a crucial question: "What should the ultimate goal of the Christian individual or organization be?"[10] I think that's a very important question. As Christians, we should not let ourselves be dazzled by the great achievements of life, but instead we should do our best to make sure our existence fulfills its mission. We're here to give glory to God, and to bring others to His feet. We live in expectation of eternity with God, and any earthly achievement is insignificant in the light of the ultimate goal, eternal life.

Many companies also face this dilemma of the wrong goals. In many organizations, institutional achievements are making it harder for the company to achieve its mission. Olga Smirnova's study evaluating efficiency and effectiveness in government transit operations is a good example of this problem. She revealed that some transit operators that were doing better in fulfilling the mission of "providing public transit to everybody who needs it" ended up forfeiting benefits for working on their mission, because the existing measures for evaluating effectiveness in transit agencies were in contradiction with the transit system's overall goal. The damage may have not been intentional but it was real.[11]

In the context of the church, it is just as necessary to evaluate whether or not we are fulfilling the mission because of which we exist as an organization. The next chapter could be defined as an introductory response to the following question: Could it be that, just like in the transit agencies Smirnova studied, some of our church's institutional achievements might be making it harder for us to fulfill the mission God entrusted us with?

The same question applies to our personal life, and all the more so. But we'll undertake that issue further ahead.

**THINK-IT-THROUGH AND APPLICATION QUESTIONS**

1. Why having a good slogan or an excellent mission statement hanging on the wall isn't enough?

.......................................................................................................

.......................................................................................................

.......................................................................................................

2. What do Matthew 7:24-27 and James 2:26 tell you about the importance of doing what God teaches us about mission, as opposed to a merely theoretical understanding?

.............................................................................................................

.............................................................................................................

.............................................................................................................

## References for this chapter

[1]Bradach, Tierney, and Stone, "Delivering on the Promise of Nonprofits", 90.

[2]See Charles Lusthaus and others, *Enhancing Organizational Performance: A Toolbox for Self-Assessment* (Ottawa, Ontario, Canada: International Development Research Centre, 1999), 65; Covey, Principle-Centered Leadership, 165, 166.

[3]Henry Mintzberg, *The Structuring of Organizations* (Englewood Cliffs, NJ: Prentice-Hall, 1979), 24, 25.

[4]Fritz, *Corporate Tides,* 88.

[5]John Sawhill y David Williamson, *"Measuring What Matters in Nonprofits",* The McKinsey Quarterly, no. 2 (2001): 98.

[6]Sawhill y Williamson, "Measuring What Matters in Nonprofits", 102, 103.

[7]Bob Dart, Big Business on Trial. *The Spokesman Review* – Feb 3, 1980.

[8]Lisa Ordóñez and others. (2009). *Goals Gone Wild: The Systematic Side Effects of Over-Prescribing Goal Setting.* Working paper for Harvard Business School. http://www.exed.hbs.edu/assets/Documents/goal-setting.pdf.

[9]Becky A. de Oliveira. Book Review—Destructive Goal Pursuit: The Mount Everest Disaster. *Journal of Applied Christian Leadership* 3(2), 67-76, p. 69.

[10]Ibid., 76.

[11]Smirnova, "Does Government Structure Really Matter?" 87.

# WHAT IS THE CHURCH HERE FOR?

MATTHEW 28:18-20 has been a classical source of inspiration among Christians to go throughout the world making disciples. The very fact that Jesus' words recorded in that text are widely known as "the Great Commission" reminds the twenty-first-century reader of the powerful influence this text has had on the missionary movement throughout history.[1] It has been argued that, "between Eden and the eternal state," few biblical topics are as important as mission.[2] In this book we have emphasized that aligning structure to mission is very important for success, whether it is in one's life, in the church, or in organizations in general. But, what is mission?

Some have questioned the legitimacy of the Great Commission as recorded in the last chapter of the first gospel, wrongly suggesting that Jesus may have never uttered those words. Some scholars see the "great commission" merely as a piece of art invented by Matthew, and others even suggest that he didn't even "invent" it, but that it was somebody else after that disciple's death.[3]

Although over two billion people in the world are Christians, that number of people only amounts to 33% of the world's population. Another 1.5 billion people (21% of the world's population) are Muslims, and believe—as strongly as Christians do, or maybe in a much stronger fashion— that their religion is the truth, and all others should convert to Islam. Over one billion people (16%) are classified as secular, nonreligious, agnostic or atheist. Hinduism boasts 900 million adherents (14%). Over 370 million people are Buddhists; and there are several other religious affiliations. In a world that is increasingly diverse and pluralistic, is it still socially appropriate to claim that Christianity has a right to go on "mission" to the entire world trying to convert all others to Christ?[4] To make things even worse, the term "mission" is not even found in Scripture as such.

And it's not just about the fact that there are several religions with global influence. There are several religions other than Christianity that have high and wonderful standards. Lay followers of the Buddhist way—for instance—often undertake five precepts: vowing not to kill, not to steal, not to have improper sexual relations, not to lie, or become intoxicated. One of the Five Pillars of Islam mandates its followers to pray at five specific moments of each day, while for Christians the frequency of prayer is a personal decision. Some people think other religions are quite as good as Christianity, or maybe even better, and that therefore it might be an absurdity and an impertinence to try to substitute one religion for the other. Mission has often been seen as "politically disruptive" and "religiously narrow-minded;" the attempt to "convert people to Christ" is sometimes rejected as an "unwarrantable intrusion," an "unpardonable interference" in people's private lives.[5]

Mission is definitely the target of countless challenges that attempt to make it disappear. And as if the realities described above were not disturbing enough, even among those who advocate for Christian "mission" there is no agreement about what mission is.

For many people, mission is preaching the gospel to one's neighbors. Others think it is primarily a matter of preaching the gospel to those who have never heard it, especially if you have to cross cultural boundaries or barriers of some other sort. Another group argues that preaching to individuals is not enough, but that churches must be planted and nourished in other cultures for mission to be really effective. Others contend that mission must include feeding the hungry, while others believe mission should focus mainly on social justice and fighting "structural sin." To complicate things even further, others think mission is simply living out a life of integrity and love and being a "silent witness."[6] Who is right?

When I travel by air and the flight attendant asks me whether I want to drink something, I often choose orange juice, and I love bringing to my kids a few of those cookies some airlines serve during the flight. But it is very clear in my mind that the purpose of an airplane is not to give away orange juice and cookies but to take people by air from one place to another. An airplane is worthless if it doesn't fly, even if the flight attendants give you plenty of delicious cookies.

Something similar happens with the church. We can do loads of activities and look good. We may treat people very well and bring good preachers and excellent musicians. We may also put up such good programs that everybody says they're really good, and we might even appear in the news sometimes. But if we're not fulfilling mission, none of those things is worth a penny.

It is very important to feed the hungry, heal the sick, and help the needy. The church certainly needs to get involved in those things. But it is also very dangerous to confuse social action with the church's mission. David Hesselgrave comments that although the biblical record in Matt. 25:31-46 has served "as a most powerful incentive to undertake a great variety of commendable Christian undertakings from digging wells to feeding the hungry to adopting orphans," the interpretation usually applied for this text to support a social gospel "is highly questionable at best."[7]

On the other hand, I firmly believe in the biblical record of the Great Commission. I love preaching about Matthew 28, and I know God has used that text to bless His church in a great many places around the world, and to inspire many to reach others. But there is plenty of evidence that the biblical mandate for global mission is much more than an isolated and contested text at the end of the first gospel. John Stott warns that, as important as the Great Commission is, Christians should not limit their understanding of mission to that text but they should rather look at the entire revelation when thinking of the missionary mandate.[8] And the Bible is full of invitations to world mission, from the first book of the Bible all the way through Revelation.

Genesis chapter 1 clearly declares that God is the creator of the entire universe, and that He is interested in living in relationship with all human beings. The answer to the problem of sin is not for one particular nation or culture, but for the whole human race. Abraham, the first cross-cultural missionary we have biblical record of, received promises of greatness, blessing and fame, followed by an explanatory note: "all peoples on earth will be blessed through you" (Gen. 12:3). The dramatic deliverance of the children of Israel from their slavery in Egypt was meant to cause God's name to be "proclaimed in all the earth" (Ex. 9:16).

God dried up the waters of the Jordan River for the Israelites to cross over, with the intention that "all the peoples of the earth" might know the hand of the Lord (Josh. 4:24). Hanna's beautiful prayer in song says that "the Lord will judge the ends of the earth" (1 Sam. 2:10). In his prayer of dedication for the temple, Solomon asked God that all those who would come to the temple to pray would receive an answer from heaven, "so that all the peoples of the earth may know your name" (1 Kin. 8:43). The book of Psalms is packed with expressions related to God's intention of having His name be glorified before all nations of the earth, and to offer His salvation to them.

The list of Old Testament references could take us several long pages. Although many have traditionally not recognized the Old Testament's contribution regarding the biblical theology of mission, several theologians have recently written on the Old Testament as an indispensable base for the church's missionary task among the nations and peoples of this world.[9]

The Gospels also have important implications for mission to the unreached. Matthew's record of the Great Commission indicates that God's witnesses were to go to "all nations" (Matt. 28:19). Mark emphasizes the need to preach the gospel "to all creation" (Mark 6:15). Luke stresses that it is necessary to evangelize "all nations, beginning at Jerusalem" (Luke 24:47).

From the Reading of texts such as these, it would be difficult to understand that being a "silent witness" or even preaching just to neighbors is enough. Johannes Verkuyl explains that, when recording Jesus' command to "go" (Matt 28:19), the author used a Greek word which means "to depart, to leave, to cross boundaries," implying that obedient disciples were to cross sociological, racial, cultural, and geographic boundaries.[10]

On the other hand, although it is very important to remember that mission implies "going" and crossing all sorts of barriers, we must also consider that it is very dangerous to "go" but do nothing of what Jesus commanded us to do. When Matthew recorded Jesus' command, he used the Greek Word πορευθέντες (*poreuthentes*, "having gone, going"), and this Word has usually been translated in Matthew 28 as "go" in imperative form. However, in the original source the word that appears in imperative is not that one but μαθητεύσατε (*mathēteusate*, "make disciples"). Simply put, Jesus' command is not as much to "go" as it is to "make disciples."

Another danger is to think that it's only about making disciples and that it's not necessary to "go," so perhaps we could focus in reaching our neighbors and forget about the rest of the world. Although the translation of *poreuthentes* as an imperative "Go" might not be the best one and perhaps it has led to an inappropriate focus on "going" rather than "discipling," if the word is not translated as a separate command but as adding emphasis and urgency to matheteusate, it then refers to making disciples for Christ, wherever they may be.[11] And in order to find those potential disciples we will often have to cross barriers that are linguistic, cultural, religious, and of many other sorts. Although making disciples is our overriding goal in the Great Commission, the church cannot just sit comfortably and wait for people to become disciples; the church also needs to "go," urgently, to make disciples to all nations.[12]

However, another issue comes up right there. The phrase πάντα τὰ ἔθνη (*panta ta ethnē*) usually translated "all nations" (Matt. 28:19), has been a source of incredible discussion. And rightly so! Speaking of the problems to understand the expression *panta ta ethnē*,

Ralph Winter complained several years ago that "the Bible rightly translated would have made this plain to us."[13] Suggesting that the classical translation of Matthew 28:19 is incorrect might seem to be a high-flown statement, but it's true.

How should we understand this text? Translating the expression *panta ta ethnē* as "all gentiles" would mistakenly make it seem as if Jesus was excluding Jewish people, and that would imply that we have absolutely no reason to work for the salvation of our neighbors or those who are already Christians, but we should only work among the "gentiles." The most common translation ("all nations") may mislead the reader to think that Jesus was talking about politically definable countries, a conclusion that would be incorrect as well.[14] When the apostle wrote the words *panta ta ethnē* he did not simply have in mind countries with political borders such as Brazil, Colombia, United States, Afghanistan, India, or Mexico. "He had in mind cultural groupings: tongues, tribes, castes, and lineages."[15]

> Suggesting that the classical translation of Matthew 28:19 is incorrect might seem to be a high-flown statement, but it's true. How should we understand this text?

When evaluating mission effectiveness, the church's focus should not be on countries but on people groups. Of course, it would be much more comfortable to think that "Christians have now fulfilled the Great Commission at least in a geographical sense," because Christianity has reached almost every politically definable country, but that is not what the Bible says. Christians need to keep active in mission until they reach all unreached people groups and make disciples among them.

John Piper suggests that Jesus' command meant the disciples should go and disciple all the ethnic groups, not merely Israel, and not even just to reach individuals: After a lengthy analysis of the usage of *ethnos, ethne,* and *panta ta ethne,* Piper concludes that "Jesus did not send his apostles out with a general mission merely to win as many individuals as they could but rather to reach all the peoples of the world."[16]

This is how Ralph Winter puts it: "In the Great Commission as it is found in Matthew, the phrase 'make disciples of all ta ethne (peoples)' does not let us off the hook once we have a church in every country—God wants a strong church within every people!"[17]

The church's effectiveness in mission, therefore, should not be judged by the number of hospitals or orphanages it has built, or even by the number of church buildings constructed or the number of baptisms achieved. Mission effectiveness needs to be evaluated in the light of the church's ability to disciple people from all people groups and establish congregations among them. Christians should be mindful that at least four-fifths of the non-Christians in the world will never have a fair opportunity to become Christians, unless Christians make cross-cultural mission the highest priority.[18]

The previous chapters emphasize that, in order to overcome oscillation between success and failure, we need to focus on mission, both individually and as a church. You need to make mission your most important priority. You need to evaluate yourself constantly and check whether or not you're fulfilling that mission. The church also needs to be periodically evaluated, and the pertinent corrective measures need to be made at all organizational levels without hesitation.

When evaluating our personal lives and realizing we fail as often as we do, we could give way to discouragement and give up the fight. An in-depth analysis of our life would certainly show that in many ways you and I are not fully aligned with mission; however, God encourages us to trust in His forgiveness and power to succeed.

Similarly, as the following chapters evaluate the extent in which the church is fulfilling its mission, perhaps someone will get discouraged and may want to give up the fight because "there are problems in the church." But such pessimistic and separatist attitude would only cause more problems and more oscillation. "Worry is like a rocking chair: it gives you something to do but it doesn't get you anywhere."[19] The answer is not in complaining and criticizing, but in doing whatever is at your hand in order to improve.

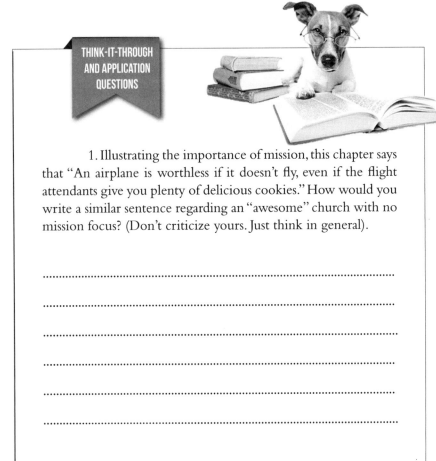

THINK-IT-THROUGH AND APPLICATION QUESTIONS

1. Illustrating the importance of mission, this chapter says that "An airplane is worthless if it doesn't fly, even if the flight attendants give you plenty of delicious cookies." How would you write a similar sentence regarding an "awesome" church with no mission focus? (Don't criticize yours. Just think in general).

......................................................................................................

......................................................................................................

......................................................................................................

......................................................................................................

......................................................................................................

......................................................................................................

2. Is it comfortable or uncomfortable for you to approach people of other backgrounds, races, or religions? How do you think a good Christian attitude in this respect should be?

..........................................................................................................

..........................................................................................................

..........................................................................................................

## References for this chapter

[1]LaGrand, *The Earliest Christian Mission to "All Nations" in the Light of Matthew's Gospel,* 235.

[2]Andreas J. Köstenberger and Peter Thomas O'Brien, *Salvation to the Ends of the Earth: A Biblical Theology of Mission* (Leicester, England: Apollos, 2001), 19.

[3]Allan Le Grys, *Preaching to the Nations,* xii; James LaGrand, *The Earliest Christian Mission to "All Nations" in the Light of Matthew's Gospel,* 236.

[4]David Van Biema, and others, "Should Christians Convert Muslims?—Religion: Missionaries under Cover", Time (2003), http://www.time.com/time/magazine/article/0,9171,1005107,00.html (accessed May 14, 2012).

[5]See John Stott, "The Bible in World Evangelization", in *Perspectives on the World Christian Movement,* ed. Ralph D. Winter and Steven C. Hawthorne (Pasadena, CA: William Carey Library, 2009), 21; John Stott, "The Living God Is a Missionary God", in *Perspectives on the World Christian Movement,* ed. Ralph D. Winter y Steven C. Hawthorne (Pasadena, CA: William Carey Library, 2009), 3.

[6]Ott, Strauss, and Tennent, *Encountering Theology of Mission,* xi.

[7]David J. Hesselgrave, "Will We Correct the Edinburgh Error? Future Mission in Historical Perspective", *Southwestern Journal of Theology* 49, no. 2 (2007): 146.

[8]Johannes Verkuyl, "The Bible in World Evangelization", in *Perspectives on the World Christian Movement,* ed. Ralph D. Winter y Steven C. Hawthorne (Pasadena, CA: William Carey Library, 2009), 22.

[9]Johannes Verkuyl, "The Biblical Foundation for the Worldwide Mission Mandate", in *Perspectives on the World Christian Movement,* edited by Ralph D. Winter and Steven C. Hawthorne, 42-48. Pasadena, CA: William Carey Library, 2009, p. 42.

[10]Ibid., 47, 48.

[11]David Bosch, "The Structure of Mission: An Exposition of Matthew 28:16-20", in *Exploring Church Growth,* ed. Wilbert Shenk (Grand Rapids, MI: Eerdmans, 1983), 230.

[12]Russell Burrill (2007). *Reavivamiento del Discipulado: Clave del Éxito en la Misión.* Doral, FL: Asociación Publicadora Interamericana, p. 21.

[13]Ralph D. Winter, "The Highest Priority: Cross-Cultural Evangelism", in *Let the Earth Hear His Voice,* ed. James D. Douglas (Minneapolis, MN: World Wide Publications, 1974), 221.

[14]James Slack, "A 'Ta Ethne' Ethnolinguistic People Group Focus as Seen in the Scriptures", paper presented for the 2003 Summer State Leadership Meeting & Church Planting Missionary Forum, http://images.acswebnetworks.com/2015/51/Slack_Ta_Ethne_Doc.pdf (accessed May 15, 2012).

[15]Donald McGavran, *Understanding Church Growth,* 3rd ed. (Grand Rapids, MI: Eerdmans, 1990), 40.

[16]Winter, "The Highest Priority", 213.

[17]John Piper, *Let the Nations Be Glad!* (Grand Rapids, MI: Baker Academic, 2010), 211.

[18]Winter, "The Highest Priority", 221.

[19]Ibid., 225.

[20]Van Wilder. Quoted by Yvonne Swinson in *Thirty-three Habits of a Really Good Man.* Springville, UT: Bonneville Books, 2010. p. 53.

## FROM THE ROCKING CHAIR TO MISSION
### PART 1

ROCKING chairs move back and forth because their structure is designed to make them move that way. If the church wants to move from oscillation to the fulfilment of mission, then we need to analyze which aspects of structure are not helping us reach that goal.

I am aware that a thorough analysis of the impact of Adventist organizational structure on mission would be an endeavor way too complex as to deal with it in just a few pages. However, this chapter and the next one represent a fairly deep introduction to such analysis, at least from 1980 to 2010. I have selected indicators such as mission giving as a percentage of tithe, the number and types of missionaries sent by the denomination throughout the years, the types of Adventist employees worldwide, baptisms and membership as measures of success, and the Thirteenth Sabbath School offering.

### Mission giving as a percentage of tithe

In the early years of the denomination, mission giving was only a small portion if compared with tithe, the first ten years showing figures between 3 and 5%. It is important to note, however, that from 1863 to 1915 a consistent (although slow) increase is evident in the World Mission Fund. From 1916 to 1935, mission giving suddenly became a very important portion of Adventist contributions, with the World Mission Fund being between 45% and 62% of tithe funds. A slow but steady decline in mission offerings can be seen from 1936 to 1979, with figures returning to 11% at the end of that timeframe.

The years 1980–2010 have seen an even more significant decrease in world mission offerings. Adventists' donations for world missions were equivalent to 10.35% of tithe in 1980, and then a consistent decline can be seen throughout the next three decades, with the exception of very small increases in just a few years during that time. In fact, world mission offerings had already decreased to 7.11% in 1990; the figure continued to go down in the next decade and reached 4.64% in 2000; finally, by 2010 world mission offerings were equivalent to only 3.78% of what a member gave in tithe.[1]

This decreasing trend has already raised concerns at the General Conference level. Robert Kloosterhuis, for instance, expressed his concern that "back in the 1930s, a person who gave 10 dollars in tithe also gave 6 dollars in mission offerings. Today, a person giving 10 dollars in tithe would give only 28 cents! I'm not a mathematician, but I'd say you can't grow a mission program worldwide that way."[2]

Although it might not be completely fair to blame the church's structure and its officers for the members' decision regarding whether or not they give mission offerings, it is to be noted that the decreasing trend is not reflected in tithe, which suggests that the message about the importance of tithe is making its way to the donors much better than the message regarding the importance of mission offering. An analysis of the numbers related to tithe per capita and world mission fund per capita would suggest the same thing.

In an organization that depends exclusively on donations to survive—such as the Seventh-day Adventist Church—, the types of contributions necessarily reflect, at least in part, the emphasis perceived by the donors as the main needs the organization aims to fill. A renewed emphasis on mission offering is necessary at all church levels. It is necessary to somehow take this message to every church member. World mission offering is not merely an option for a denomination that aims at reaching every tribe, tongue, and people with the gospel message.

### Number and types of missionaries sent abroad

In 1979, the Seventh-day Adventist Church started recording the number of active interdivision employees (which is the traditional name for missionaries in Adventist polity), with 1,561 of them. That figure remained fairly stable between the years 1980 and 1984, and then a slow decline can be seen from 1985 to the present. As of December 2010, the Seventh-day Adventist Church had only 860 interdivision employees.

Instead of growing throughout the years as the denomination expanded, the number of missionaries has seen a reduction of 44.9% in those 31 years.[3] Has the need for missionaries declined or are there other factors leading to the decreasing number of missionaries in the denomination?

Although it is difficult to deny the tremendous advances of Christian mission in the recent 100 years, 7,162 of the 16,594 people groups in the world (43.2% of them) have not received the gospel yet;[4] the percentage of people groups reached with the Adventist message is obviously much more worrisome. On the other hand, by 2010 a total of 2,252 language groups did not even have one verse of Scripture in their own language, and very few people were working to solve that problem.[5] It is very evident that the need for missionaries has not declined. The decreasing trend in the number of missionaries sent, therefore, should receive serious consideration, both from local church members and from church leaders worldwide. We should not fall into the trap of blaming church administrators, partly because missionaries can only be sent by the General Conference provided that there are enough financial resources, and the mission offerings we the members give have been declining in a significant way over the years.

The next question would be, what have been the assignments given to Interdivision missionaries throughout all these years? Although no information is currently available for the years 1980-1998 regarding missionary assignment, the General Conference's

Secretariat office sent me for this study a general report covering the years 1999 to 2012. The report was published in my doctoral dissertation, and it is available through Andrews University.[6] It is impossible to insert those fifty pages here (and it would be really boring, I guess), but a summary will surely be appropriate here, and it's going to be easier to understand.

During the years 1999-2010, the General Conference reported a total of 3,093 missionary (Inter-Division Employee) assignments. From that total, 1,063 assignments were classified as educational (top leaders from educational institutions, teachers, librarians, principals, girls' or boys' deans, etc.). The number of medical assignments was 629 (nurses, physicians, hospital managers, etc.).

There were 28 assignments to publishing organizations (printing house managers, editors, etc.), and 142 pastoral/evangelistic assignments (Bible workers, church planters, local church pastors, chaplains, etc.). A total of 855 were classified as "others" in conference/ missions organizations (office administrative secretaries, conference/ union/division presidents, treasurers, department directors, etc.), and 376 worked with the Adventist Development and Relief Agency (ADRA).

Looking at these data in terms of percentages is much more revealing. From 1999 to 2012, most of the missionary assignments (34.3%) were for educational work, the second largest category was some type of administrative capacity in conferences or missions organizations (26.6%), the third largest one was the medical category (20.3%), the fourth was ADRA (12.1%), the fifth was the pastoral/ evangelistic category (4.5%), and the sixth was the publishing category. One particular thing stands out as a significant concern: The pastoral/ evangelistic category is second-to-last in missionary assignments from 1999 to 2012.

It is clear that something is wrong. As I explained in chapter 5, members pull organizations in different directions depending upon their role in the company, their personal interests, and other factors.

A similar thing is happening in the Seventh-day Adventist Church. Jerald Whitehouse contends that although the General Conference Secretariat was entrusted with the task of administering foreign mission, "instead of acting like a mission board, strategizing, and directing work for unreached peoples, the secretariat has functioned more as a department for interchurch aid, filling the needs of the existing institutional structure."[7]

As Bruce Bauer and Lester Merklin suggested in 2007, those places where the Adventist message has been preached for some 100 years should provide local budgets for teachers and institutional workers currently funded with Interdivision Employee (IDE) budgets so that present IDE budgets can be steadily shifted to the 10/40 Window "until at least 63% of Adventist missionaries work where 63% of the world's population lives."[8]

It is easy to blame the General Conference for this problem. However, we should not forget that the church's leaders at the global level cannot get this done without every Division and local field being convinced of the urgent need to refocus IDE budgets to reach the unreached. Perhaps it will even be necessary for IDE budgets to be transferred from the divisions to the General Conference for assignment.

On the other hand, although it might be encouraging to see Adventist missionaries raising the educational level of people, taking good care of the church and its institutions, healing the sick, and improving the lives of the needy, it is an issue of concern that the pastoral/evangelistic category has been anything but a priority in the assignment of Interdivision employees in the Seventh-day Adventist Church.

It is worth pointing out, however, that Adventists are not alone in this trend. For example, it is estimated that 73.1% of foreign missionaries are being deployed to places with access to Christian witness and where most people would say they are Christians. Another 24.5% of missionaries are sent to places where people have access to Christian witness although many have not decided to become Christians. Only 2.4% of missionaries are serving in places where most people are not Christians and do not have access to a Christian witness. Simply put, only 2.4% of the missionaries who are being deployed to foreign fields are actually working among the 1.6 billion people who have not had a chance to hear the good news of the gospel.[9]

I want to highlight two other important matters: Adventist Volunteer Service and the Global Mission Pioneers program. The Seventh-day Adventist Church has volunteers serving in 66 countries under direct supervision of the General Conference, plus many others travelling on their own.[10] The Global Mission Pioneers program, started in 1993 by the Global Mission initiative, has provided a small stipend for tens of thousands of volunteers who have ventured into areas with no Adventist presence and planted new groups of believers. It could be argued that this initiative is the major reason why the denomination has tripled its membership since 1990.[11]

When the Global Mission Pioneers program was established in 1993, there were 832,087 Adventists in the 10/40 Window nations. By 2010, the number was 2,845,308. In that period, global membership had grown from 7,962,216 to 16,923,239. In other words, from 1993 to 2010 the denomination's growth rate was around 249% in the 10/40 Window, while it was only 97.5% in other parts of the world, and growth rate for the global church as a whole was 112.5%.[12] These statistics are consistent with the concept that, when lay members are enabled for ministry and are given tools to develop it, mission is accomplished in a faster and more efficient way.

Adventists utilize a high percentage (68%) of their Global Mission Pioneers in the least evangelized parts of the world, which is indeed a very positive thing. According to Bauer and Merklin, however, half of these pioneers are working in only two countries, and they contend that "further research would show that most of these are not reaching peoples within the great world religions, with the exception of no-caste Hindus."[13] David Trim explains that even though church leaders are no longer sending as many missionaries and church members are not giving as much to foreign missions, the church is growing more rapidly in the 10/40 Window than in the rest of the world. The potential for success is enormous. I wonder what would happen if church members would wake up to the need of giving more offerings for world mission, and if administrators would send more resources and personnel to unreached areas such as this one.

### Types of employees

Another interesting indicator in the present study is the number of evangelistic workers as compared with the number of institutional workers the denomination has hired throughout the years.

In 1863, only 30 workers were reported, and all of them were classified as evangelistic. There were 72 evangelistic workers in 1870, 260 in 1880, 411 in 1890, and 1,500 in 1900. Up to this point, no reference is made in the statistical reports to "institutional" workers. There were 4,346 evangelistic workers in 1910 (52% of the total) and 3,918 institutional workers (47%). In 1920, a total of 13,081 workers were reported, 6,955 of them evangelistic (53%) and 6,126 institutional workers (46%). In 1930 there were 10,988 evangelistic (51%) and

10,473 institutional workers (48%). The percentage of evangelistic workers continued to decrease in the following few decades, while the percentage of their institutional counterparts continued to increase. The 1970 report indicated that the denomination had twice as many institutional workers as evangelistic workers. Institutional workers constituted 66% of the total in 1980 and 71% in 1990, while evangelistic workers were only 33% of the total in 1980 and 28% in 1990. The 1993 Annual Statistical Report stopped categorizing workers as either evangelistic or institutional, and started categorizing them as either general or institutional instead. In 2010, institutional employees numbered 138,713 (62%) while general employees numbered only 82,047 (37%), even though that number included primary school teachers along with evangelistic workers in the general category.

As confusing as the previous statistics may seem, at least one thing is clear: The percentage of evangelistic employees has been decreasing while the percentage of their institutional counterparts has been increasing throughout the years in the Seventh-day Adventist Church. This suggests that, at least in this area, the structure has not been allocating its resources in alignment with its mission.[14] Some would argue that institutions are missional but, as Michael Cauley warns, "the Adventist Church was not organized merely to be the custodian of an organizational system, to control and maintain institutions."[15]

> **THINK-IT-THROUGH AND APPLICATION QUESTIONS**

1. How worrisome do you think the decrease in Interdivision workers is? How can every church member help solve this issue?

...................................................................................................................

...................................................................................................................

...................................................................................................................

2. Michael Cauley says that "the Adventist Church was not organized merely to be the custodian of an organizational system, to control and maintain institutions." What do you think of such warning?

...................................................................................................................

...................................................................................................................

...................................................................................................................

# References for this chapter

[1]Statistics from this section have been taken from the 31 editions of the *Annual Statistical Report* published by the Seventh-day Adventist Church from 1980 to 2010.

[2]General Conference of Seventh-day Adventists Office of Adventist Mission, 2009, "The Rumor", video presented to the Annual Council of the Executive Committee, http://www.youtube.com/ watch?feature=player_ embedded&v=8MLW3pXssfs (accessed January 19, 2013).

[3]Secretariat Office, "Annual Council Agenda and Support Material" (Silver Spring, MD: General Conference of Seventh-day Adventists, 2011), 34, 35.

[4] Joshua Project, "All Progress Levels", http://joshuaproject.net/global-progress-scale.php (accessed March 26, 2013).

[5]Paul Eshleman, "World Evangelization in the 21st Century", http:// joshuaproject.net/assets/articles/essential-elements-of-great-commission.pdf (accessed March 26, 2013).

[6]Abraham Guerrero, "Structure and Mission Effectiveness: A Study Focused on Seventh-day Adventist Mission to Unreached People Groups Between 1980 and 2010" (Ph.D. dissertation, Andrews University, 2013), 207-256.

[7]Jerald Whitehouse, "Developing New Church Structures for More Effective Mission, Nurture, and Growth of Believers", in *Adventist Responses to Cross-Cultural Mission,* ed. Bruce Lee Bauer (Berrien Springs, MI: Department of World Mission, 2006), 51.

[8]Bruce L. Bauer y Lester Merklin, "The Unfinished Task", *Journal of Adventist Mission Studies 3,* no. 1 (2007): 40, 43.

[9]Global Frontier Missions, "State of the World", http://www. globalfrontiermissions.org/stateofworld.html (accessed March 27, 2013).

[10]G.T. Ng, "Membership Dilemma: Promise and Peril", Secretary's report to Annual Council, Silver Spring, MD: General Conference of Seventh-day Adventists, 2011.

[11]General Conference of Seventh-day Adventists, Office of Adventist Mission, "Global Mission after 20 Years", http://www.adventistmission.org/ frontline-2010-2q-feature (accessed January 20, 2013).

[12]Secretariat Office, "Program & Agenda—2012 Annual Council" (Silver Spring, MD: General Conference of Seventh-day Adventists, 2012), 60.

[13]Bauer y Merklin, "The Unfinished Task", 33.

[14]Abraham Guerrero, "Structure and Mission Effectiveness: A Study Focused on Seventh-day Adventist Mission to Unreached People Groups Between 1980 and 2010", 165, 166.

[15]Gina Wahlen, "100 Years of Mission Giving - Making a World of Difference", *Adventist World* 8, no. 11 (2012): 17.

# FROM THE ROCKING CHAIR TO MISSION
## PART 2

THE previous chapter explored mission offering as a percentage of tithe, the number and types of missionaries sent by the denomination throughout the years, and the types of Adventist employees worldwide. The present chapter analyzes the Thirteenth Sabbath School offering, the number of baptisms and members as measures of success in mission, and the Adventist Church's global strategy.

## The Thirteenth Sabbath School Offering

Since the first Sabbath School mission offering was collected in 1885 by the Upper Columbia Conference in the United States to send missionaries to Australia, this offering has become a mission-oriented tradition for the Seventh-day Adventist Church. The following year, the General Conference promoted the construction of the mission boat Pitcairn, the Sabbath School mission offering became a global initiative, and the thirteenth Sabbath of each quarter was selected for this new plan.[1]

I have published elsewhere a detailed table analyzing all mission projects from 1980 to 2012, indicating the world Division or region that quarter was dedicated to, the description of each project, and its classification (for established work/ possibly for mission to new areas /clearly for reaching the unreached). Although such information is very valuable, that table took thirteen pages, so I decided to summarize it in the following five-line table.

Table 1

*Thirteenth Sabbath School mission projects (1980-2012)*

| Period | For established work | Possibly for mission to new areas | Clearly for reaching the unreached | Totals |
|--------|------|------|------|------|
| 1980–1990 | 81 | 29 | 5 | 115 |
| 1990–2000 | 63 | 46 | 44 | 120 |
| 2000–2012 | 105 | 32 | 10 | 147 |
| Totals | 249 | 107 | 26 | 382 |

I wouldn't take those five lines lightly. During that 32-year period, 382 major projects have been promoted and have received support of the Adventist Church worldwide through the thirteen Sabbath offering. The fact that a worldwide denomination had come together to support almost four hundred major projects in only three decades is quite impressive!

However, as it is the case with all other areas of life, there's room for improvement here as well. Out of the 382 projects promoted during those three decades, 249 were clearly aimed at strengthening established work, 107 could be classified as possibly for mission to new areas, and only 26 were clearly directed towards reaching the unreached. In other words, 65.2% of the projects announced for the Thirteenth Sabbath School Offering from 1980to 2012 was directed towards building the church where it already existed, 20% had evangelistic and mission potential but no specific focus on new territories, while only 6.8% of the projects clearly focused on taking the Gospel to the unreached.[2]

While it is true that the church needs to strengthen its presence in many parts of the world, these statistics suggest that the missionary focus of Thirteenth Sabbath School projects like the Pitcairn in 1886 has been partially obscured by the organizational needs of the church.

## Number of baptisms and members as measures of success

The future looked bright for Angie, who just eight months before had been hired to teach in the Faculty of Mathematics, and had just bought a new car and a house. Her students really loved her, and she was happy with their academic development. As she stepped out of the classroom one afternoon, she bumped into the University's academic dean, who had been looking for her. "Angie, I urgently need to tell you something. Got a minute?"

A few moments later, as she walked towards her car in the parking lot, tears came out of her eyes. The dean's words were still ringing in her ears, "I'm worried about you. You need to publish at least one article before finishing the school year, otherwise you will not pass the evaluation and we'll have to let you go." Angie could have qualified as the perfect teacher, but doing research and getting published wasn't very easy for her. Now, her career was suddenly at risk.

She's not the only one. Research expectations for college teachers are higher and higher, to the extent that doing research and getting articles and books published has become the dominant criterion —and sometimes the only one—for hiring, tenure, and promotion of college professors.[3] Although studies have repeatedly pointed out that a good researcher is not necessarily a good teacher, the push to reward researchers keeps rising in educational institutions. Even if it is unintentionally, many administrators mismanage reward systems because they hope employees will be motivated toward a particular goal, but they reward something else.[4]

Could it be that a similar situation is happening in the Seventh-day Adventist organization? David Trim's study of mortality rates in the Seventh-day Adventist Church's thirteen global divisions compared to mortality rates in their own regions could help answer that question.

Official Adventist records reported 4,424,612 Adventist members at the beginning of 1985 and 119,997 deaths during the years 1980-1985 (5.26 deaths per thousand); interestingly, however, the global mortality rate was 10.20, which makes Adventist mortality look much smaller than global mortality. A similar pattern can be traced as a consistent trend for the years leading to 2010.[5]

Although Seventh-day Adventists have historically been known for their healthy lifestyle and longevity, the huge difference between Adventists' officially reported mortality rates and those of the global community cannot be attributed solely to a healthy lifestyle. David Trim explains that it is possible to reach a rough estimate "applying global mortality rates (from UN data) to SDA membership statistics." His estimate would indicate that there are almost half a million unreported deaths in the denomination's records from 1980 to 1996, and over a million from 1980 to 2010.[6]

What does all of this have to do with Adventist structure and mission? In Adventist polity the influence of a particular field in the global decision-making process is highly influenced by membership size,[7] and it is through baptism or profession of faith that individuals are added to church membership. In other words, Adventist reward systems seem to encourage pastors and regional administrators to help people make their decision to follow Christ and join the church, but the system has no significant rewards for following up with anything that happens to believers after baptism.

Official reports indicate how many members the local congregation or field has, but not how many discipleship programs are taking place or how many cross-cultural mission efforts are being undertaken. The pastor who develops a discipleship program with church members but doesn't have a good number of baptisms goes unnoticed and in some fields runs the risk of being seen as somebody who is not efficient, just as the college professor who teaches very well but is not very good at writing articles and books.

Arguing that Adventist pastors and/or administrators are inflating the membership numbers to get more voice and vote would be unfair, because there is no clear evidence for that. But it is clear that current church policies do not encourage discipleship, but just baptism. Current policies don't encourage accurate reporting of those who left the church or died either, and that fact could explain the difference between Adventist mortality rates and those of the general population. In fact, an administrator who suddenly cleans the records in this respect will probably find his or her field underrepresented in the next upper-level meeting.

Just like university managers who expect professors to be excellent teachers but reward research instead, it is possible that Adventist global leadership assumes and expects pastors and regional administrators to focus on mission (making disciples, reaching the unreached) but the reward system emphasizes something else. Baptizing is just a little part of the Great Commission.

Remember those professors who spend more time in teaching preparation than in research and often go unnoticed? It might be difficult to admit it, but just like them, pastors who focus on mission may not be as well rewarded as those who spend more time and effort on increasing the numbers that receive more attention in the Annual Statistical Report and in all other organizational meetings.

In a seminar for pastors and families, Alejandro Bullón told the attendees that one day his local field president approached him worried because he had heard that 70% of the pastors in their field have lost their dream, their vision, and their motivation. As a result of that conversation, a study was conducted in South America in order to discover why. The company that outsourced the project collected data from questionnaires, the Church Manual, the Working Policy, and many historical documents, knowing nothing about the church before. According to the report, the research team concluded that the denomination's organizational structure is like a pyramid with most people at the very bottom, fewer people in the next upper level, and so on, until the highest position, that of the world church's president.

Bullón drew the imaginary pyramid and explained what the researchers said, "By what we infer from the questions that have been answered among your pastors, all those who are down here [at the bottom of the pyramid] have only one dream: to get up here [to the very top of it]." Although pastors laughed when elder Bullón said those words, he continued to convey the researchers' conclusions: "After a few years of struggle to get up here [to top of the pyramid], they see their dream slip farther away every day. And that's the end of it all. They will finish their 40-year work with no more dreams."[8] Although I have not found enough support for these researchers' statement about the Seventh-day Adventist organization, this story by elder Bullón is a valuable reminder of the fact that it is mission and nothing else what has to be the ultimate goal of every church member and pastor.

### The Adventist Church's Global Strategy

An outstanding element indicating a positive influence of structure on mission in the Seventh-day Adventist Church is what came to be known as Global Mission, and such initiative needs to be highlighted here. At the Annual Council of 1986, Neal C. Wilson, then president of the General Conference, called for church leaders to develop a global strategy for reaching the world's unreached. A few years later, on the morning of October 10, 1989, the denomination's Annual Council voted to approve a document called Global Strategy of the Seventh-day Adventist Church. The document, also endorsed at the 1990 General Conference session, formally introduced the concept of "people groups" to the denomination and in several other aspects marked a significant turning point in the history of Adventist mission.[9]

By that time, however, the General Conference's world divisions and attached unions had gathered extensive information in response to Wilson's call and had adopted the idea of "population segments," a concept that would eventually prevail over its "people groups" counterpart in organizational measurements within the church.[10]

The Global Strategy approved in the 1989 Annual Council clearly stated that "evangelizing target populations will be most effective if they are divided into people groups, whose group characteristics facilitate a group approach in evangelism and secure decisions for the gospel."[11] However, the lack of specific information regarding the number of people groups and the fact that it was difficult to evaluate progress in that respect caused church leaders to adopt an alternate plan, as described below.

### The "1-million-population-segment approach"

In 1989, some analysts within the church divided the world into "population segments," defined as non-overlapping geopolitical territories of the world, each occupied by between half a million and a million and a half persons as of mid-1989. The 1989 Annual Statistical Report published a table with each division's number of such population segments, members per thousand people, population segments with no Adventist churches or companies, and some other facts.[12] Thus, the General Conference had formally proposed in October 1989 to establish by the year 2000 a Seventh-day Adventist presence in every population segment of one million as identified at the beginning of the decade 1990-2000, and some work in each of 271 languages spoken by one million or more people.[13]

Of necessity, the 1989 table of unreached population segments was incomplete. By 1990, the church reported 2,248 1-million-population segments with no churches or companies, and clearly set as the church's goal at that time "to see that all 5,257 population segments in the world have a company or a church."[14] The years 1991 and 1992 saw the Annual Statistical Report printed with no report on the total number of unreached population segments. For 1992, 83 segments were reported as "entered since 1990," 179 segments for 1993, and 240 for 1994.

In a slightly different format, the following year's report announced that 14,295 "targets" had been chosen within 1-million-population segments since 1990, and that 6,772 had been entered by 1994. The same report showed 15,450 targets chosen and 8,170 entered by 1995. By 1996, the number of "chosen targets" was reduced to 13,464 and 5,780 of them were reported as entered. The reporting format was changed again in 1997 and the population segments disappeared. The challenge of Global Mission to place a church among each one million of earth's population has been continually reaffirmed since 1990 in every year's issue of the *Annual Statistical Report* at the beginning of Global Mission's section. However, there has been no consistency in showing whether or not a church had been established in each of the 5,257 segments identified in 1990.

In spite of the lack of consistency in the church's official reports regarding the 1-million-population segments, some leaders still remember the goal and track the church's progress on it. In a 2005 article, G. T. Ng talked about 2,300 groups of one million people without an Adventist presence (an amount slightly different from the 2,248 reported in the 1990 *Annual Statistical Report*), and he added that by 2001 only 460 of those population blocks remained without Adventist presence. If the 1-million-population-segment approach is still going to be used, it is necessary for accountability to track and report where the church is in relation to the segments identified in 1990, and to update the goal by considering changes in population patterns.

The "unreached people-groups" approach

The other option would be to focus on people groups rather than blocks of a number of people who might be separated by impressive barriers. However, there are pros and cons in this approach. A major advantage is that the church would be much more faithful to the God-given mission to make disciples of all people groups, not just of all politically definable countries.[15]

A major disadvantage is that this approach is much less encouraging than the traditional approach and would require a shift "from self-congratulation to championing the needs of the unreached."[16] By focusing on countries, for instance, the Seventh-day Adventist Church was able to report in 2010 that the denomination's work had been established in 209 out of 232 countries and areas of the world recognized by the United Nations. For the superficial reader, this might suggest that the church's mission is almost accomplished, because there are only 23 unentered countries or regions. This approach, however, ignores the multiple types of barriers that divide those countries.

The concerns expressed in 1989 regarding the fact that different categories of people groups are overlapping and constantly changing continue to be true today. However, there is more information available now regarding people groups than in 1990, which could facilitate a more informed decision in the Seventh-day Adventist Church, and would make it more feasible to develop plans to reach specific people groups and make disciples among them. And, considering the importance for the church to embrace such a task, it is not acceptable for the denomination to be content with reports on Adventist congregations planted among million-population-blocks while remaining unclear about the degree in which the church has been reaching and discipling unreached people groups in the 10/40 Window and elsewhere.[17]

**THINK-IT-THROUGH AND APPLICATION QUESTIONS**

1. What do you think church administrators can do to encourage discipleship and not only baptisms? ¿What can you do to help others become disciples?

..............................................................................................

..............................................................................................

..............................................................................................

..............................................................................................

2. With the pressures of modern life, many people get carried away with their job, studies, and a lot of other things, to the extent that they can't make time to share Jesus with their friends and other people. What can you do to make mission your ultimate goal?

..............................................................................................

..............................................................................................

..............................................................................................

..............................................................................................

..............................................................................................

# References for this chapter

[1]Gina Wahlen, "100 Years of Mission Giving - Making a World of Difference", *Adventist World* 8, no. 11 (2012): 17.

[2]It is worth noting that These percentages reflect only the information published in the *Sabbath School* and *Mission* quarterlies and available at the time of this research, and do not indicate the projects's size or the actual amount of money budgeted for each project. For the fourth quarter of 1980, for instance, 500 rural churches were grouped by the Trans-Africa Division in a single project while for the third quarter of 1990 the Africa-Indian Ocean Division grouped only 7 churches in a single project.

[3]Michael Prince, Richard Felder and Rebecca Brent. Does Faculty Research Improve Undergraduate Teaching? An Analysis of Existing and Potential Synergies. *Journal of Engineering Education* 96(4), 283-294 (2007), p. 283.

[4]Ashkenas and others, *The Boundaryless Organization,* 100.

[5]For the years 1986-1990, there were 4.42 deaths per thousand in the Adventist Chuch, while global mortality rate was 9.60. Adventist mortality rate for the years 1991-1995 was 22.14 per thousand, but global mortality was 46.50. For the years 1996-2000 Adventists reported 21.05 deaths per thousand, while global mortality rate was 45.40. During the years 2001-2005, 3.56 deaths per thousand were reported in the church, but global mortality rate was 8.60. For 2006-2010, 3.23 deaths per thousand were reported, while global mortality rate was at 8.50. See David Trim, "Office of Archives Statistics and Research," in *Membership Dilemma: Promise and Peril*—Secretary's Report to the Annual Council (Silver Spring, MD: General Conference of Seventh-day Adventists, 2011).

[6]Trim, "Office of Archives Statistics and Research".

[7]Note, for instance, that different fields are given the privilege of having one, two, or three delegates to a General Conference session according to their status (union conference/union mission, union of churches conference/union of churches mission, local conference/local mission), and then each division is entitled to additional delegates based upon its membership as a proportion of the world Church membership. Each division distributes its quota of delegates to the unions affiliated with that division, based on each union's proportion of the division membership.

[8]Alejandro Bullón, "El Mensaje y el Mensajero", 2013, Audio recording of a seminar for pastoral families, http://www.southernunion.com/article/359/ministries/ministerial/ministerium-2013-seminars (accessed March 27, 2013).

[9]See General Conference of Seventh-day Adventists, "Minutes of the Meetings of the General Conference Committee, Annual Council" (Silver Spring, MD: General Conference Secretariat, October 10, 1989), 392, 472, 473.

[10]Office of Archives and Statistics, *127th Annual Statistical Report,* 2.

[11]Ibid.

[12]Ibid., 40.

[13]General Conference of Seventh-day Adventists, "Minutes of the Meetings of the General Conference Committee, Annual Council", Meeting of October 10, 1989.

[14]See Office of Archives and Statistics, *127th Annual Statistical Report,* 2, 40; Office of Archives and Statistics, 128th Annual Statistical Report, 43-46.

[15]See McGavran, *Understanding Church Growth,* 40; Winter, "The Highest Priority: Cross-Cultural Evangelism", 221.

[16]Jerry Chase, "A Voice from the Back Seat", *Journal of Adventist Mission Studies* 1, no. 1 (2005): 89.

[17]General Conference of Seventh-day Adventists, "Minutes of the Meetings of the General Conference Committee, Annual Council", Meeting of October 10, 1989.

# TOO MANY ARMS AND LEGS?

THE LITTLE boy was exhausted. He had certainly enjoyed his long walk through the jungle with dad, but now it was very late, the path started to look rather dark, and the shadows of the jungle scared the child. As bad as daddy wanted to take his child home as quickly as possible, he eventually realized they would have to stay overnight in the middle of nowhere.

The experienced man of the countryside lay down on his back in a plain area by the river and invited the child to join him to sleep, assuring the kid everything would be fine. And it was so, at least for a while. But as unfamiliar sounds growingly filled the night, the frightened little boy crawled in between his father's legs, his little head resting on dad's belly.

Before long, a hungry tiger came down to the river and, smelling humans, quietly walked around sniffing everywhere. When he got to the father and his son, he was barely able to identify what was in front of him. As the child's head was hidden in the deep shadows of his dad's belly, what the tiger saw in the dusky night made him think he had lost his senses.

"One, two, three, and four arms… One, two, three, and four legs… That's too many arms and legs for a human body!" the tiger thought to himself. "I have never seen anything like this." Suddenly, as the feline came closer smelling up and down the body of that strange creature, he sniffed so close that his huge whiskers tickling the man's nose made him awake sneezing a big "ah-ah-ah-choooo!"

Taken by surprise, the massive tiger fell backward into the river, making a huge splash. By the time he was able to get out of the water, father and son had jumped up and hurried away. When Martha Hamilton and Mitch Weiss tell this popular story from Malaysia, they end up saying that "to this day the tiger probably thinks he was seeing things that night, for he never again saw the creature with four legs, four arms, and only one head that let out a big Ah-Ah-Ah-CHOO!"[1]

## The "other parts" of the body of Christ

I know this is just a story, but I'm afraid some of it can happen in real life, even at church.

I was raised in a Seventh-day Adventist home, and my parents taught me that the church is Christ's body (1 Cor. 12:12-31). I also read that the health message is the right arm of the work, and that health reform needs to be given its place in official church business, at home, and elsewhere in life so that "the right arm will serve and protect the body."[2] Today, however, I woke up before the crack of dawn with one question in mind: If the medical missionary work is the right hand of the church, what are the other parts of the body of Christ?

When he was 24 years old, my dad quit his career and a bulky paycheck in order to engage in colporteur ministry, convinced as he was that "in a large degree" it is through the publishing work that God's people will accomplish "the work of that other angel [of Revelation 18] who comes down from heaven with great power and who lightens the earth with his glory."[3] My mom has been a teacher in Adventist schools for her entire professional life, and her efforts in founding more schools and cause them to prosper have always been inspired by her deep belief in the importance of educational work as a part of what the church is supposed to do.

But the medical missionary arm of the church and the educational arm are not the only limbs in the body of Christ. For 2011, Adventists were broadcasting through 1,989 radio stations and

1,525 T.V. stations each week; the denomination was administering 2,068 educational institutions beyond elementary school, 20 food industries, 172 hospitals and sanitariums, 169 retirement homes and orphanages, 236 clinics and dispensaries, 14 media centers, and 62 publishing houses and branches.[4]

A not-so-easy-to-track number of unofficial institutions needs to be added to the list of arms and legs within the church, since a myriad of employees and 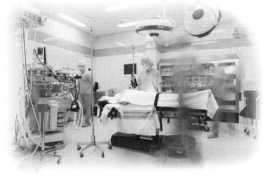 volunteers are currently working for lay-led semi-autonomous organizations throughout the world. Can the Seventh-day Adventist Church really manage all those fields of labor effectively or, perhaps, in our effort for doing so much we are simply doing nothing? As the hungry tiger in front of the strange creature in the Malaysian story, sometimes I wonder if maybe there are too many arms and legs in the body of Christ.

If James White had heard my concern in 1871 he would have replied with a sounding no. Having been one of the most important leaders in the process of shaping the Seventh-day Adventist Church structure, he wrote on October 24, 1871, in the Review and Herald, "Our people are well organized. Our Church Organization, State Conferences, General Conference, Systematic Benevolence, and Publishing organizations can hardly be improved. To say the least, the machinery works well."[5] Barry Oliver notes that when the Seventh-day Adventist Church was organized in the early 1860s, those involved in the process thought that their model was so adequate to the needs of the church that it would never need revision. "Within twenty-five years, however, there were indications that revision of their plan was indeed necessary."[6] A major reorganization of the administrative structures of the Seventh-day Adventist Church took place between 1901 and 1903.

The satisfaction expressed by James White about the Seventh-day Adventist Church's structure a few years after the organization of the denomination is remarkable. However, times and circumstances have changed, and the structure that was so useful for that era may not be the most suitable for the twenty-first century. Several concerns have been raised regarding the need for a revision of structure, especially in terms of how it may impact the church's mission effectiveness.

George Knight, for instance, published a book entitled The Fat Lady and the Kingdom in which he illustrated the issue of structure and mission in Seventh-day Adventism by creating his own "parable of the fat woman" in the context of Matthew 13. His parable suggests that "the church is like unto a fat woman returning from a shopping spree."[7] Knight explains that "we now have a bureaucratic structure which appears to be limiting our achievement of mission in some serious ways. Administrators breed administrators and even in times of financial crisis it is hard to decrease their numbers."[8]

> Several concerns have been raised regarding the need for a revision of structure, especially in terms of how it may impact mission effectiveness.

Bruce Bauer agrees that Adventists need to analyze the current impact of structure on the mission of the denomination. He argues that "church organization and structure can impact the mission and ministry of the church either positively or negatively. However, there is a tendency to just continue to work within the structural and organizational form that was inherited from the past rather than doing the hard work of analyzing and deciphering the exact needs of the present."[9]

### Evaluating the problem and its possible solutions

In 1997, two neurologists and a neurosurgeon reported the case of a 64-year-old, left-handed woman in Switzerland who, after experiencing weakness and abnormal skin sensations in her left leg with no apparent cause, underwent surgical extirpation of a right parietal parasagittal meningioma. Two days after surgery, the patient reported

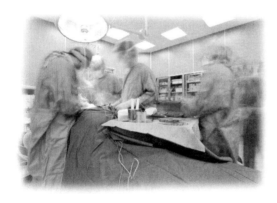

she had a continuous, uncontrollable feeling of having 4 legs attached to her body. She felt two legs lying on the right side, and the other two on the left side. "I know it is not possible to have 4 legs, so I know it cannot be true," the patient recognized. But according to the physicians, sometimes she was so confused she just had to double-check by touch or sight.[10] Although the feeling of supernumerary legs in this woman was continuously present for 14 days, it had completely disappeared on the 15th day after surgery.

In George Knight's parable, perhaps the problem of structure can be solved by simply dropping some of those bags the lady got in her shopping spree. If we were trying to learn lessons for the church from the popular Malaysian story, we could think the problem is simply a fantasy and we don't have to worry or get scared as the tiger did. If the problem of church structure is like the illusory feeling of extra legs in the report of that lady in Switzerland, in a few days the illusion will fade away and everything will get back to normal.

But the church cannot just "drop the bags" it has acquired in the form of so many departments, attached institutions and semiautonomous organizations it carries on its shoulders. It is impossible, in the blinking of an eye, to get rid of the organizational machinery and the myriad of employees we have to support financially. It would be a self-delusion to say the problem of structure is not real and, like the tiger, the only thing we have to understand is that our scare was just a misunderstanding. The many additional arms and legs the body of Christ seems to have in the Seventh-day Adventist Church are not just going to disappear in 14 days. Does this puzzle have a solution, or do we need to yield to the criticism of those who suggest we have to leave the church?

First of all, if the answer to structural problems to focus on mission, that's just what we have to do. I've seen too many groups out there concerned that the church's organizational structure doesn't work as it's supposed to, or disappointed for the alleged lack of consecration to God in some of our leaders. And I don't blame them. There are things that are worth being concerned about. However, the devil's most frequent temptation for those who spot failures within the church is that he pushes them to leave, and too many people fall into that trap.

**Fixing Noah's Ark from inside**

Most of the time when I hear about Noah's ark, it's the beautiful part that is stressed: Bystanders watch in awe as animals of many sorts suddenly arrive and line up to get into the ark, as if a mysterious hand were guiding them. The patriarch preaches his last sermon and gets into the huge wooden structure, obedient as he was to God's command. An invisible hand shuts the ark's door before the astonished eyes of its eight new dwellers. When the rain comes, God's powerful hand protects the ark as the rest of the world is shattered into pieces. Amen!

True. The story is beautiful. But it does have another side, not so nice. Have you ever wondered what Noah and his family felt like after an entire day of heat inside the ark, with no sign of rain coming down? Can you imagine the cruel mocking of people outside the ark three days after the door had been shut? Can you guess what the ark smelled like after seven days of strong heat, especially if you think all those animals were inside? Sometimes we forget that, although being within the ark was certainly a privilege, the eight human beings who dwelled in it may have experienced plenty of revulsion there more than once.

I'm not sure how to explain what specific animals entered the ark, because the Bible doesn't give too many details. However, the biblical record does say that there were at least "two of every kind" (Gen. 6:20). I can only imagine how horrible it must have been to stand by the skunk (also called polecat) when he felt threatened by the heavy storm or because some animal came too close to him. The skunk's typical foul-smelling spray should have been especially disgusting if you consider there was no way to get fresh air.

But even if I'm wrong and the skunk wasn't there but some type of ancestor representing his "kind" instead, the smell shouldn't have been any nice. Furthermore, all kinds of animals were represented in the ark, and of course they might have been pooping, peeing, and farting as they normally do (as gross at it might sound). The ark was completely closed, and I wonder what the air smelled like after a few weeks of storm.

In many ways, the church is like the ark. While it is true that we find salvation in Christ and refuge within the church amidst the heavy storm in this sinful world, it is also true that sometimes there are situations among God's people that seem to be as disgusting as some of the stinky smells in Noah's ark. You may know church members who don't study the Bible and don't pray either. You may know deacons who are not very kind with kids, or treasurers who think they own the church. Perhaps you've had a really bad experience with a pastor or local elder who doesn't seem to reflect Christ's passion for the lost soul. You might be disappointed because you think the church's structure is way too heavy and it's hindering the fulfillment of mission. You may even know somebody who has left the church and joined an independent movement that handles their tithe and offerings by themselves, and they think they can do better than the church.

Just imagine what would have happened if Noah's sons, desperate about the situation I described, had stepped out of the ark. Within the ark, they had to endure the heat first and then the nerve-racking combination of disgusting smells, but they would have died outside. Perhaps the ark's constant movement and everything else may have caused more than one to vomit, but at least they were safe from the storm. Any attempt to fix the ark from outside would have ended up in disaster and death.

I think it's worth repeating it. In many ways, the church is like the ark.

**THINK-IT-THROUGH AND APPLICATION QUESTIONS**

1. What does "fixing the church from inside" mean to you?

..................................................................................

..................................................................................

..................................................................................

..................................................................................

..................................................................................

2. What can you do to "drop the bags" that sometimes hinder you from fulfilling mission?

..................................................................................

..................................................................................

..................................................................................

..................................................................................

..................................................................................

# References for this chapter

[1]Martha Hamilton and Mitch Weiss. *Through the Grapevine: World Tales Kids Can Read & Tell.* Little Rock, AR: August House, p. 77.

[2]Ellen White, *Counsels on Health,* 434.

[3]Ellen White, *Publishing Ministry,* p. 5.

[4]Office of Archives, Statistics, and Research, *2013 Annual Statistical Report,* pp. 5-7.

[5]James White, "Our Machinery", *Review and Herald* 38, no. 19 (1871), http://www .adventistarchives.org/docs/RH/RH18711024-V38-19__B/index. djvu (accessed January 28, 2009).

[6]Barry David Oliver, "Principles for Reorganization of the Seventh-day Adventist Administrative Structure, 1888-1903: Implications for an International Church" (Ph.D. dissertation, Andrews University, 1989), 67.

[7]George R. Knight, *The Fat Lady and the Kingdom: Adventist Mission Confronts the Challenges of Institutionalism and Secularization* (Boise, ID: Pacific Press, 1995), 15.

[8]Ibid., 49.

[9]Bruce L. Bauer, "Editorial", *Journal of Adventist Mission Studies* 3, no. 1 (2007): 3.

[10]Patrik Vuilleumier, Alain Reverdin, and Theodor Landis. Four Legs: Illusory Reduplication of the Lower Limbs After Bilateral Parietal Lobe Damage. In: *Archives of Neurology* 54(12): 1544.

## ROCKING CHAIRS OF DIFFERENT SIZES

I WILL call her Esther. I can only imagine her shock-like face right after she finished the demographic questionnaire and the personality one. As the instructor finished reviewing the questionnaire's results with her, he made a long pause. Then he looked directly into her eyes and read what he said were the results of the personality test: "You are the type of person who is going to end up alone later in life. You may have friends and relationships now, but when you get to your mid-20s most of them will have drifted away. You may even marry or have several marriages, but these will probably be short-lived and are very unlikely to continue into your 30s. Relationships won't last, and when you're past the age where people are constantly forming new relationships, the odds are you'll end up being alone more and more."[1]

### A one-person rocking chair

The first thing I want to mention in this chapter is an individual, self-centered rocking chair that for no reason can hold more than one person. It might be a person who thinks it makes no sense to share Jesus with their friends or anyone else. Perhaps it's someone who believes in the necessity of witnessing for Christ, but he or she feels it's just too hard for them to do. Let me say it clearly right now: We were created to live in relationships, and those relationships are meant to bring glory to God. Anyone who tries to live a life that is completely independent and isolated from everybody else is condemned to rock back and forth in the rocking chair of life and will never get anywhere worth the trip.

Ester, the girl in our story at the beginning of this chapter, was part of a group of 140 people who were unknowingly participating in a study on social exclusion and self-defeating behavior.[2] Those who were told they were going to end up alone in life showed greater tendency to take irrational risks, although it was evident that their decisions were against themselves and would expose them to more problems.

In another experiment with 259 participants, certain psychologists manipulated the situation in a similar way, and they found that those who were exposed to believe they were going to end up

alone in life or that other participants had rejected them, were less willing to donate money, serve as volunteers or cooperate with others.[3] Another study with 187 individuals found that those who were told they were going to end up alone in life experienced a reduction of their intelligent thought.[4]

These studies and several others suggest human beings cannot live just for themselves and yet feel completely fulfilled. Although different societies form marriages in different ways (often strikingly different!), all known societies have family and marriage as a common element. It would be impossible for a society or civilization to exist without any sort of interaction among its members. Structure, then, is necessary in all cultures. Human beings need structure in order to survive. There are groups, families, businesses and other organizations, societies, churches and schools. Every single one of those organizations is made up of people, and responds to the same inherent need in human beings: the need to establish relationships.

When God created human beings, He made them in need of relationships. And He was very intentional in having Adam realize that. The Bible says Adam gave names "to all the livestock, the birds in the sky and all the wild animals," but he noticed that there was nobody around "suitable" for him (Gen. 2:20). What God said out loud that day about the issue has already become a very popular statement: "It is not good for the man to be alone" (Gen. 2:18). It looks like God was giving Adam a message that was supposed to be received by the rest of the world as well.

Furthermore, the very act of creating Adam involves more than one person in Deity. "God said, "let us make mankind in our image, in our likeness" (Gen.1:26). Although we may never fully understand the mystery that there is only one God yet we are talking about three different persons, the triune nature of God is evident even from the biblical record of creation. Somebody described it by saying that creation of humanity "is the one act in the whole creation drama that calls for community action."[5]

When you share Christ with others, you are improving the quality of your life. You are approaching the ideal for which God created you. As we discussed earlier, human beings were created in God's image, and for His glory. "None of us lives for ourselves alone" (Rom. 14:7). Therefore, by focusing on mission and sharing Jesus with others, you are simply becoming a better person. And that's one of the major blessings of belonging to a church, by the way. You are strengthening your ability to live in relationships, and if you're focused on mission you're attracting others to your circle of Christian relationships. Through that process, you grow in Christ.

**Two other rocking chairs within the church**

Every now and then I hear the complaint that independent ministries work better and bring about more results than the church's organizational structure. And now that I've written a book that says the church is like a rocking chair, I'm pretty sure I'm going to hear more people complaining. Many church members stop giving their offerings—and even their tithe—to the church in order to give them to such independent organizations instead, because they seem to do the work best. Is it worth it?

The church's two structures

Between 1970 and 1974 Ralph Winter introduced the idea that the church has two types of structures, which he called modality (congregational structure) and sodalities (mission structures). Winter argued that the church's efforts will be most successful when both structures are fully and appropriately involved.[6]

Highlighting the fact that in the times of Apostle Paul his missionary band (sodality, or mission structure) specifically nourished the churches (modalities, or congregational structures), Winter insisted that such friendly and mutually-supporting relationship is a most significant symbiosis. Sadly, however, church history is full of moments in which these two structures have not had a very good relationship.[7]

What is a "congregational structure"? In simple words, it is the structure of a given denomination, (including local churches and the denomination as a whole). In the context of the Seventh-day Adventist Church, the term includes local churches and companies, local conferences/missions/fields, union conferences/missions, unions of churches, and the General Conference with its regional divisions.[8]

A congregational structure usually has the following characteristics:[9] (1) it has a multifaceted concern and an overfull schedule; (2) the majority of its programs are inward orientated, with an emphasis on those who have already accepted Christ as their Savior; (3) its programs are oriented towards consolidation rather than towards initiation, by either increasing the size of existing

congregations or starting daughter congregations without attempting to take the gospel to cultures where there is no Christian church, or as Blincoe puts it, growing the church "where it already is;"[10] (4) it usually moves slowly because it invests in building consensus; (5) it provides longevity and continuity, giving members a sense of unity, stability, and security; (6) it is people-oriented (most of the finance and personnel of the church are committed to the nurture and service of members); (7) it works as a check and balance to help regulate activities and set policies; and (8) it tends to be authoritarian and to dominate, often refusing to recognize mission structures and their roles, even if they are legitimate.

Now, what is a mission structure? The term refers to task-oriented, mission-focused organizations within the church or working in association with it. In the context of the Seventh-day Adventist Church, a "supporting ministry" that is focused in mission could be considered a mission structure.[11]

Mission structures usually share the following characteristics:[12] (1) their resources and efforts are usually concentrated into one small, narrow area in order to reach their objective; (2) their leaders are more concerned with initiation than with consolidation, thus tending to grow the church in unreached areas and often crossing cultural, linguistic, and geographic boundaries rather than focusing on the local congregation; (3) while congregational structures are people-oriented, mission structures are task-oriented and their leaders usually show a low tolerance for unproductive people; (4) they are usually started and guided by charismatic leaders; (5) since mission structures more often cross cultural barriers, their leaders are more innovative and open to change; and (6) they usually have less stability and a shorter life than the congregational structure.

The Seventh-day Adventist Church's organizational structure is built on the following elements as its primary building blocks: the local church, the local conference/mission, the union conference/

mission, and the General Conference. That was very easy to write, and it fit in just a few lines, but it represents a tremendous organizational machinery with over two hundred and twenty thousand employees. In a study on church structure, Lowell Cooper acknowledged that the Seventh-day Adventist Church has seen in its ranks "a rapid and widespread development of independent supporting ministries" in the most recent decades. He also noted that although such organizations represent an "enormous blessing," it is also true that church members' support to such structures reflects "uncertainty regarding the effectiveness or efficiency of denominational structure to get the job done."[13]

**Tension between the two "rocking chairs"**

In 2005, Ralph Winter and George Miley wrote a brief article each, both related to the necessity of establishing support ministries for missions (or mission agencies). They decided to put their articles together under the same title: "Who needs mission agencies? (and who needs local churches?)"[14] When I read the title, I couldn't help but laugh. After the laughter, though, I thought it through. It's really sad that there's so much division within God's people.

In fact, rivalries between a denomination's organizational structure and its independent ministries are so big that they're already considered normal among Protestants. But the unhealthy tension between denominational structures and independent ministries is not only a sad reality among Christians in general, but also specifically within the Seventh-day Adventist Church. Many who are affiliated with independent ministries harshly criticize the church's organizational structure, while church leaders also throw their darts against independent ministries.

As he was leading a workshop on mission, the professor noticed a hand being raised among the students, asking for a chance to speak. Unaware of what it was all about, he allowed the comment, and then he was shocked at what he heard from the lips of that sincere church pastor who could not hold expressing his dissatisfaction with independent ministries. He complained, even as he knew some of them are focused on mission and remain loyal to the church: "I'm sick and tired of mission agencies coming to rape our poor church." This pastor was complaining about the money that independent ministries ask for in the church. But of course this is only one of several other reasons why many people do not like these semiautonomous ministries.

On the other hand, it is also true that many independent ministries do not like the denominational structure at all. They accuse the church of having fallen in excessive bureaucracy and apostasy. They say the denomination wastes in administrative positions the money that could be given to lay people so they do the work. Occasionally, Seventh-day Adventist history has even seen some suggesting that organization is so evil that the church needs no structure other than the guidance of the Holy Spirit.

Does it make sense that official church leaders and the representatives of independent ministries continue to fight against each other? Obviously, it doesn't. And let's remember that structure is not the problem, but the lack of consistency in aligning with mission everything we do. As Lowell Cooper put it, "organizational structure is necessary—and it must be portrayed as complementing mission rather than competing with it." [15]

The Bible would be clearly against an attitude that is unwilling to accept structure at all, because everything should be done "in a fitting and orderly way" (1 Cor. 14:40). Common sense would also be against this attitude, especially considering the fact that our Adventist family includes over 17 million people around the world. Giving up the structure that holds us together as people in a mission would imply, humanly speaking, to disappear.

Anthropological studies would also stand against the initiative of throwing away our organizational structure. Social relationships and structures are universal, and they are also inherent to human nature; societies need organization to survive. Missiological studies suggest that mission agencies or independent ministries, no matter how mission-focused and successful they may seem, need the church's continuity and longevity, and they also need much of the church's structural machinery in order to survive. Churches, on the other hand, need the dynamism of supporting ministries in order to prevent stagnation and fulfill mission, even if they have to make it through barriers of different sorts.

This being the case, it makes no sense for us to fight against each other, because we need each other. It makes no sense to overlook structural concerns either. Although the church should avoid focusing so much in organizational matters that loses its focus on mission, it is impossible to ignore the various issues of structure and yet be faithful to the mission God entrusted us with.

### Who does it better?

It's Saturday morning. Someone stands up there in your church in front of everybody and speaks about the great achievements of his mission agency. Emphasizing that the group is loyal to the Adventist organization and instead of accepting tithe they send their own to the church, the group's leader presents a report of how his organization has been working in the 10/40 Window, planting churches and building schools for the last five years.

The congregation shudders to think that this little group of "rebels" who are loyal to the church have been able to do in such little time what the denomination was unable to do in several years. Offerings rain down for the mission agency on that day. Ten years later, for some reason the mission agency that performed so well no longer exists. However, the church is still there, and one of these Sabbaths another person will come to the front and speak about a new mission agency that needs prayer and financial support.

Talking about this situation, Lowell Cooper warned several years ago:

> In many cases independent supporting ministries report significant programmatic accomplishments that may even overshadow what seem to be the accomplishments of the regular denominational structure. What is not always so clear is that many independent supporting ministries also rely heavily on church infrastructure rather than creating such infrastructure for their own needs.[16]

And, if they want to remain loyal to the church, they cannot create too much of an independent infrastructure! At the end of the day, the church needs supporting ministries, and they need the church.

As I was writing my doctoral dissertation, I reviewed several studies about various types of organization, looking for  ideas to help explain or solve this historic tension between the church and independent ministries. It was interesting to realize that "independent ministries"[17] have also become very common outside of the context of the church, under names such as "special-purpose governments," "private organizations," and a few other names.[18]

In the world of organizations, there is plenty of research in this area, and an application of all that would suggest that there is no clear evidence that independent ministries do the job in a way that is more efficient or more effective than the organized church. To complete the picture, it also seems to be impossible to prove that the church's official structure can do the work better than independent ministries. I guess it's evident that we shouldn't be fighting against each other, but helping each other fulfill our God-given mission!

Woodrow Whidden contends that the Seventh-day Adventist Church, "from its highest levels down to its local churches," has developed a lengthy and successful history of engaging mission structures "in mutually affirming ways that have produced surprisingly

little schism."[19] But it would be difficult to deny the conflict that characterizes the relationship between many independent ministries and the church's formal structure.

Ralph Winter explained in 1970 that society has all kinds of free enterprises that are not administered by the government, from philanthropic foundations to money-making manufacturing and service industries. In a similar way, he explained, the church needs to allow for semi-autonomous structures under its jurisdiction but not directly administered by the denomination.[20]

Over four decades later, the government/industries illustration is still alive in conversations about the two structures. Winter suggests that dynamism in the church substantially rests on the existence of a good relationship between the denomination or modality as a regulator and the mission structure or sodality as something like a private enterprise or non-governmental organization. Denominational governments should monitor supporting ministries and provide "quality control" for them in the same way that governmental entities monitor private industry. These ministries or mission agencies, in turn, should keep focused on mission and loyal to the church, complying with its guidelines.[21]

We may spend our entire life arguing with independent ministries, and they may waste their time trying to show how inefficient church structure might be. But continuing with this debate is just another distraction that takes us away from mission. A much more productive option would be for the denomination's official leadership to foster a healthy relationship with the many semi-autonomous structures which continually appear within its ranks. On the other hand, leaders and supporters of such supporting ministries should focus on fulfilling the church's mission rather than wasting time and energy in criticizing the denomination's structure while many who have not been reached with the Gospel are perishing without hearing the good news of the gospel.

I have already said, very clearly, that in many ways the church oscillates back and forth just like a rocking chair. It's hard to deny that in front of the evidences out there. However, those who criticize the church so harshly should remember that, in many ways, independent ministries oscillate as much as the church itself or even more. In other words, if the church is like a rocking chair, independent ministries are indeed rocking chairs as well, only smaller. Instead of fighting against each other, the organized church and independent ministries should work together for the good of mission.

THINK-IT-THROUGH AND APPLICATION QUESTIONS

1. Do you think it makes sense for independent ministries and the organized church to work together to fulfill mission? What are some cautions both sides need to remember?

........................................................................

........................................................................

........................................................................

........................................................................

........................................................................

........................................................................

........................................................................

........................................................................

........................................................................

# References for this chapter

[1]Jean M. Twenge, Kathleen R. Catanese, and Roy F. Baumeister, "Social Exclusion Causes Self-Defeating Behavior", *Journal of Personality and Social Psychology* 83, no. 3 (2002): 609.

[2]Ibid, 606-615.

[3]Jean M. Twenge and others, "Social Exclusion Decreases Prosocial Behavior", *Journal of Personality and Social Psychology* 92, no. 1 (2007):56-66.

[4]Roy F. Baumeister, Jean M. Twenge, y Christopher K. Nuss, "Attitudes and Social Cognition—Effects of Social Exclusion on Cognitive Processes: Anticipated Aloneness Reduces Intelligent Thought", *Journal of Personality and Social Psychology* 83, no. 4 (2002):817-827.

[5]Zac Niringiye, "In the Garden of Eden—1: Creation and Community", *Journal of Latin American Theology* 5, no. 1 (2010): 25.

[6]For Winter a modality is a structured fellowship in which there is no distinction of sex or age, while a sodality is a structured fellowship that requires an adult second decision beyond modality membership, and is limited by either age or sex or marital status. According to this definition, both a national or global denomination and the local congregation are modalities, while a mission agency or a local men's club are sodalities. See Ralph Winter. Two Structures of God's Redemptive Mission." *Missiology* 2, no. 1 (1974): 121-139.

[7]Winter also complained that in the early post-biblical period a healthy New Testament relationship between modality and sodality was not as usual. Then sodalities became very significant during the medieval period within Catholicism, but were basically ignored by Protestants from the beginning of the Reformation until the times of William Carey, when they were rediscovered.

[8]See General Conference of Seventh-day Adventists, *Working Policy* 2011-2012, 53-54.

[9]For a deeper study on the characteristics of the church as a structure, see Bauer, "Congregational and Mission Structures", 13-17; George Miley, *Loving the Church—Blessing the Nations: Pursuing the Role of Local Churches in Global Mission* (Waynesboro, GA: Authentic Publishing, 2003), 88, 141; Pierson, *The Dynamics of Christian Mission,* 36.

[10]Robert Blincoe, "The Strange Structure of Mission Agencies. Part I: Still Two Structures after All These Years?" *International Journal of Frontier Missions* 19, no. 1 (2002): 6.

[11]A "supporting ministry" is defined in the Seventh-day Adventists' Working Policy as an independent organization with the following characteristics: (1) its leaders and representatives are members of the Seventh-day Adventist Church, and  support the denomination's goals and purposes, positively supplementing with their work "that of the Church in carrying out the gospel commission;" (2) its theological positions shall be in harmony with

the fundamental beliefs of the Seventh-day Adventist Church; and (3) the organization does not accept tithe but its leaders "shall encourage their supporters to be faithful in returning tithe and appropriate offerings through the authorized channels of the Seventh-day Adventist Church. See General Conference of Seventh-day Adventists, *Working Policy,* 2011-2012 ed. (Washington, DC: Review and Herald, 2011), 385.

[12]Bauer, "Congregational and Mission Structures", 20-24; Blincoe, "The Strange Structure of Mission Agencies, Part I", 5; Miley, *Loving the Church— Blessing the Nations,* 74, 88.

[13]Lowell C. Cooper, "Reasons for Considering Adjustments to Seventh-day Adventist Church Ministries, Services and Structure", http://www.adventist. org/world-church/commission-ministries-services-structures/cooper-reasons-for-considering.html (accessed August 27, 2013).

[14]Ralph Winter y George Miley. Who needs mission agencies? (and who needs local churches?) *Mission Frontiers 27(3),* pp. 8-9.

[15]Lowell C. Cooper, "Reasons for Considering Adjustments to Seventh-day Adventist Church Ministries, Services and Structure".

[16]Ibid.

[17]Abraham Guerrero, "Structure and Mission Effectiveness: A Study Focused on Seventh-day Adventist Mission to Unreached People Groups Between 1980 and 2010".

[18]Special-purpose governments, also referred to as special districts, are autonomous local governments that provide a single service (or limited services), in contrast with general-purpose governments, which are responsible for a wide range of public services and have wider authority than special-purpose governments. Kathryn A. Foster. *The Political Economy of Special-Purpose Government* (Washington, DC: Georgetown University Press, 1997); Olga Victorovna Smirnova, "Does Government Structure Really Matter? A Comparison of Efficiency and Effectiveness of Special Purpose Versus General Purpose Government Transit Operations" (Ph.D Dissertation, The University of North Carolina at Charlotte, 2008).

[19]Woodrow W. Whidden, "The Adventist Church and Independent Ministries", *Ministry* 73, no. 8 (2000): 18, 19.

[20]Winter and Beaver, *The Warp and the Woof,* 56.

[21]Robert Blincoe, "The Strange Structure of Mission Agencies. Part I: Still Two Structures after All These Years?" *International Journal of Frontier Missions* 19, no. 1 (2002): 6.

# HOPE FOR THE CHURCH

### AMIDST CRITICISM

CRITICISM against the church is not a new thing, but now it's more trendy than ever. Allan Machado points out that for so many it is already normal to do *church shopping* (looking around for a church that meets my needs, tastes, and even desires), *church hopping* ("jumping" from one church to the other without committing to any church for a significant period of time, because "it no longer fills me"), and *church dropping* (not simply switching churches, but stopping church attendance and stay home watching appealing preachers online or on TV if anything).[1] People in our days tend to get discouraged when they spot imperfections or anything they don't like in the church, and many just leave.

Although many of the concerns regarding the church are valid, the attitudes I just mentioned are not exactly what the church needs for good change to happen within it. "Remedies" such as faultfinding, finger-pointing, and separatism are not the answer either. In fact, they are worse than the disease itself. It's all about Jesus and the mission he entrusted us with. We must make mission our highest priority, and the issue will fade away.

Now, you might be thinking you can't change the church, but that's not true. I have come to realize that real change happens in the church when its members raise awareness of the issue, and not merely when leaders push a reform, as good as those administrative initiatives can be. Real change starts from the member level, not from the "top" level.

Sure, we can't make decisions for the General Conference regarding how many missionaries are going to be deployed next year, or what would be the budget for the Global Mission Pioneers initiative. However, if we don't push ourselves and others to start giving more mission offerings, church leaders will never be able to send more missionaries or approve more Global Mission projects. Most of us certainly are not in a position to re-focus the 13th Sabbath School Offering to reaching the unreached, or to decide how much money will be set aside for evangelism in our local Conference, but we can make a personal list of 5-10 friends we want to help get closer to Jesus, and start being intentional about making it happen. We can make mission-focused decisions in our personal lives and, if most members do so, the church will just have to follow the pace.

Instead of finger-pointing, let's praise God for those who approved the 1989 Global Strategy of the Seventh-day Adventist Church. Let's hail God for the boldness of the General Conference in investing so much money in the Global Mission Study Centers and the Mission Institute, which have increased Adventists' ability to understand world religions and reach them with our message. Just as Aaron and Hur held Moses' hands up when he grew tired, let's pray for the General Conference president and his team, and also for every Division officer, church pastor, and lay leader, and for the myriad of loyal supporting ministries around the world, that the Lord might use them all for the good of mission.

Remember Bernie, the Adventist pastor who went public about his struggle with porn? I always wondered why he was so intentional in making it public. And I also noticed that his story has led thousands to realize that Jesus Christ is the true source of freedom. So I approached him and asked him whether a sense of mission had anything to do with his recovery. What he told me in his February 2014 email both shocked me and reaffirmed my faith in the power of mission:

Just a few years ago… I was going through a particularly difficult time of struggling to maintain sobriety. I couldn't believe how the old urges had returned and I was feeling tempted and vulnerable. It was in that season that God really spoke and revealed that I had lost a sense of purpose and mission. I was still speaking around the country and sharing my story but clarity and conviction about the bigger purpose/mission had slipped into the background.

Bernie's recovery was all about mission. He had done everything in his hand to get away from porn, yet the rocking chair of life was horribly real for him. And it wasn't until his encounter with a deeper sense of his God-given mission that he found real freedom. Reflecting on all that he has gone through, Pastor Bernie told me, "There's no question that a clear sense of mission is absolutely essential for me to remain sober… In fact the reason we tend to cope with life's challenges in unhealthy ways is often because we lack a deep sense of mission and purpose."

I don't know what it is that you're struggling with. Perhaps you've been fighting with bad eating habits, or you haven't been able to stop smoking or drinking. It might be a secret sin only God and you know. Maybe you're active within the church yet it feels like you haven't been able to cultivate a really meaningful relationship with God. Perhaps you're within the church, but lost.

If you are sick and tired of the seemingly endless cycle of sin and repentance, the answer is mission. God wants to set you free from evil, and He also wants you to reflect His glory to others so they can know God's freedom too. By the well, the Samaritan woman found not only forgiveness in Jesus, but also a deep sense of mission, and as a result many people made their way to Jesus (John 4:28-30). The Gadarene man who had been demon-possessed begged Jesus to let him stay with the Savior who had just healed him, but only to receive the command to go on a mission to spread the news about the Lord (Mark 5:18-20). When Jesus healed a leper and strictly warned him not to tell anyone, the thankful man "began to talk freely, spreading the news," and people came to Jesus "from everywhere" (Mark 1:45). Some found that the more Jesus commanded them not to tell anyone, "the more they kept talking about it" (Mark 7:36, 37). When your life is mission-driven, you will no longer rock from success to failure and back again. Your path will be "like the morning sun, shining ever brighter till the full light of day" (Prov. 4:18).

### An "angel" who's not an angel

It was 7:15 in the night when they gave me the microphone to preach. I had a remote control in my other hand, and after praying I asked all those in the audience to slowly raise their right hand and pretend they had a remote control as well. I guess the only thing I didn't do was giving every church member a little bag of popcorn.

We counted to three out loud and then everyone was supposed to turn on the TV with their remote. When we said "3", the following Bible text appeared on the church's big screen: "Then I saw another mighty angel coming down from heaven. He was robed in a cloud, with a rainbow above his head; his face was like the sun, and his legs were like fiery pillars" (Rev. 10:1).

That's how it all starts. It's one of my favorite prophecies in the Bible. Revelation 10 portrays a mysterious character with an impressive shape, holding an open little book in his hand, and his voice like the roar of a lion. Verse 1 describes in full detail the mysterious character. The rest of the chapter is devoted to showing some sort of top-quality feature film in which thunders don't make noise but speak clearly, and the screen is so interactive that the viewer is able to step in and take up a role in the movie.

There's no other part in the Bible where an angel is given so much attention. The word used in Rev. 10:1 to talk about this character is αγγελον *(angelon),* which means "messenger," and may refer to a human being who carries a message, as well as to a supernatural being such as angels or even God himself.[2] In the entire chapter, that mysterious character is the central figure. Who could that "angel" be? Some of the character's traits can help us know his identity.

The angel's feet are described as similar to "fiery pillars" and he was "robed in a cloud" (Rev. 10:1). Pillars of fire and cloud were the same two symbols God employed to guide the people of Israel day and night, respectively, in their journey from Egypt to Canaan (Ex. 13:21, 22). Let's be reminded that when Jesus comes, we will see Him "coming on the clouds of heaven" (Matt. 24:30). On the other hand, the rainbow on the angel's head was the same symbol God used as a "sign of the covenant" between Him and the earth right after the flood (Gen. 9:11-13), and also the same symbol He used in a vision given to Ezequiel the prophet to represent "the glory of the Lord" (Ezek. 1:28), and the same thing that "encircled the throne" where the King of the universe was sitting in another vision (Rev. 4:2, 3).

About the "angel," it is also said that his face was "like the sun" (Rev. 10:1), which brings to mind the description of Jesus in Rev. 1:16. Also, the Old Testament talks about Jesus as the "Sun of righteousness" who brings salvation or healing "in his wings" (Mal. 4:2, KJV), and this is the same Jesus who wanted to gather his children as a hen gathers her chick "under her wings" (Luke 13:34). The fact that the "angel" of Rev. 10 is shown with his face "like the sun" also seems to be a reference to the symbol Jesus used to portray Himself before his disciples on the mountain of His transfiguration (Matt. 17:1, 2).

Just in case anyone has a doubt regarding who the "angel" of Rev. 10 is, this chapter's central figure gives a loud shout "like the roar of a lion" (v. 3), the same symbol used for Jesus, the "Lion of the tribe of Judah" (Rev. 5:5). Furthermore, Jesus Himself warned that we should not swear "either by heaven, for it is God's throne; or by the earth, for it is his footstool" (Matt. 5:34, 35). However, we see here somebody who is swearing "by him who lives for ever and ever, who created the heavens and all that is in them, the earth and all that is in it, and the sea and all that is in it" (Rev. 10:6). Who could do that with such authority, and receive so much attention instead of being penalized?

All these characteristics point to only one person. It's just like putting together the different pieces of a puzzle. When you're

about to finish, you're finally able to catch the whole picture. It's as if, through many symbols, the entire Bible were repeating that the mysterious character of Rev. 10 is not an angel, but Jesus, dressed like an angel.[3] And it should not come as a surprise that Christ portrays Himself as an angel in Rev. 10, because the biblical record shows more than once that Divinity takes the form of an angel, such as in the cases of Genesis 16:7-14 (Hagar); 22:11-18 (Abraham); 31:11, 13 (Jacob); 32:24, 28, 30 (Peniel); Exodus 3:2 (Moses); Judges 2:1 (Bokim); 13:3 (Samson).

God Himself confirmed the identity of this mysterious character of Rev. 10 when he revealed that "the mighty Angel who instructed John was no less a personage than Jesus Christ."[4] But why wouldn't Jesus send the message of Rev. 10 with an angel? Didn't Gabriel the angel do his job well when he took Mary the message that she would be Jesus' earthly mother? What other message could be more important or fragile than that one, so that Jesus wouldn't entrust it to anyone but He rather decided to dress up like an angel and delivered it Himself?

While Jesus is the main character in Rev. 10, that chapter's central message revolves around the little book Jesus holds in His hand. Which one would that book be? The Greek Word which is used to describe what Jesus was holding in His hand is βιβλαρίδιον *(biblaridion),* a diminutive form of βιβλίον *(biblion),* which means "book." *Bibliaridion* refers to a little papyrus scroll, and is translated as "little scroll" (Rev. 10:2), so it can't be the same book as the one in Rev. 5, since *biblion* is the word used there, which evidently refers to a bigger book.

Something that can help identify Rev. 10's "little book" is the fact that in the drama of chapter 10 the author insists that the little book was "open" (vv. 2, 8). Jesus broke away with all the pre-established schemes by presenting Himself glorious in this scene and by swearing by all that represented His authority that "there should be time no longer" (v. 6, KJV). Why would Jesus insist so much that the little book was open, even stating in such a sensitive swearing with all the emphasis He could do it, that "there should be time no longer"?

Regarding Daniel's visions related to the 1,260-day prophecy (Dan. 12:7, 9; 7:25) and the 2,300-day prophecy (Dan. 8:14, 26), the biblical record tells us that these prophecies would be sealed up "until the time of the end," when "knowledge" shall increase so these prophecies could then be understood. Now, in Rev. 10, Jesus decides to personally deliver the message that a certain "little book" is "open," and He insists with an extremely categorical swearing that "there should be time no longer."

If you carefully analyze Jesus' swearing in Rev. 10, you will notice the scene is very similar to prophet Daniel's vision in which a "man clothed in linen" is holding up both of his hands to heaven and also pronouncing a solemn oath. The evidence is strong that Rev. 10: 5-7 is a reference to Dan. 12:4-7.

The book that had been sealed is now open. Its message needs to reach all corners of the planet. Daniel's prophecies, sealed "until the time of the end," were opened to be understood right when "there should be time no longer;" when the prophecies of Daniel 8-11 come to their end and there would be no more time prophecies.[5]

Every time I review Revelation 10 it seems more splendid to me. And it's even more impressive to see that just when the "time of the end" came, God touched the hearts of people around the world to study prophecies as never before.[6] Such a message was not preached in previous centuries. But "since 1798 the book of Daniel has been unsealed, knowledge of the prophecies has increased, and many have proclaimed the solemn message of the judgment near."[7]

It is impossible to examine Rev. 10 word by word in such limited space as this chapter. But I do want to mention a few more issues that catch my attention: first, the command to eat the little book in spite of the fact that it would first be sweet and then bitter (vv.8–10); and second, the command to prophesy again in spite of the bitter experience (v. 11).

I don't know about you, but if I'm warned that a particular food is going to be sweet in my mouth but after I eat it it's going to be bitter in my belly, I definitely wouldn't eat it. I'm impressed by how John, obedient to Jesus' command, goes to Him, asks Him for the little book, and eats it: "Then I took the little book out of the angel's hand and ate it, and it was as sweet as honey in my mouth. But when I had eaten it, my stomach became bitter" (Rev. 10:10).

Many people studied during that time the advent message, savored it, and preached it with passion. But the message that was first sweet would become very bitter. The case of Charles Fitch just strikes me. He was an outstanding Presbyterian minister who accepted the Advent message and preached it with a lot of enthusiasm, becoming one of the most beloved Adventist preachers of his time.

During a cold October day of 1844, Fitch went to the lake in order to baptize a big group of people. At the end of the ceremony, he stepped out of the water in his wet clothes (they had no protective baptismal robes back then), and started his way back home amidst the typically cold wind of that season. But just then a second group of baptismal candidates was approaching, and Fitch came back into the water to baptize them, shivering as he was because of the cold wind. Then he baptized a third group that came on the last moment, driven as he was by his belief that Christ was about to come. But this was already too much for him. The brave preacher died from pneumonia on October 14. His last words were "I believe in the promises of God."[8]

Charles Fitch's experience is just a little taster of the pain Millerites experienced when, after preaching with all their strength and longing with all their hearts for Jesus' coming on October 22 1844, the day went by and Jesus didn't come. Pain pierced the hearts of believers as bad as a deadly spear. Sometime later, certain Millerites saw their disappointment explained in Rev. 10, a prophecy of their own experience.[9]

When I read Rev. 10 in its context, I feel grateful to God for having called me to be part of the Adventist movement. Out of the ashes of the great disappointment Millerites endured, the Lord plucked out a little brand, a flame of faith that now sheds light over more than 200 countries around the world: the Seventh-day Adventist Church. Just as God prophesied in that chapter, a worldwide movement was born at the beginning of the end of time, in order to preach Daniel's prophecies and announce Christ's second coming. The Seventh-day Adventist Church is not merely another denomination, but an organization that was born directly out of a biblical prophecy. Praise God!

After John's bitter experience with the little book, Jesus approached the apostle and warned him that "you must prophesy again about many peoples, nations, languages and kings" (Rev. 10:11).[10] It sounds like Jesus is telling His people, "I know it hurts, but you need to focus on mission." The same chapter that predicts the emergence of the Seventh-day Adventist Church and therefore it gives us so much certainty that our church is not merely another denomination but a prophetic movement founded by God Himself, also gives us a tremendous invitation to mission. What a timely message!

Sadly, it is very easy for the church to prophesy "about" many peoples, nations, languages and kings and yet neglecting the mission of reaching them with the everlasting gospel. We may find ourselves healing the sick, teaching, refining our theology, constructing religious buildings, developing projects that add a "good image" to the church (not that there's anything wrong with that), but while we are preaching to ourselves millions die without hearing this beautiful Third Angel's message.

It is even possible to report a high number of baptisms and pat ourselves in the back, congratulating ourselves for "fulfilling mission" while we cover our eyes to the reality that most of those new converts were already Christians from other denominations or even rebaptisms, and we're not doing very much for those who haven't even heard the name of Jesus in their own language. As G.T. Ng said in October 2013 to the global Adventist Church's Annual Council attendees, "sometimes statistics have a way of massaging the ego." We pastors, administrators, professors, and other Adventist leaders definitely need to focus on mission.

> There's enough biblical support for staying within the church in spite of it all. Christ Himself took the form of an angel in order to remind us that He was the One who founded this church.

On the other hand, those who tirelessly criticize the church would also do well in focusing on mission and stop wasting their time in fault-finding. Many people become too easily disappointed when they discover faults in church leaders or when the church doesn't meet their expectations. But we need to remember that there's enough biblical support to believe we need to stay within the church in spite of it all. Christ Himself took the form of an angel in order to give us the precious message that He was the One who founded this church.

**Three solid reasons to be a Seventh-day Adventist**

Although there are plenty of additional reasons to be faithful to the Lord within the organization God Himself founded to be His church and to preach this message, I have chosen the three characteristics by which James Nix defines our church. I strongly believe they are three very strong reasons to be faithful to God within the Seventh-day Adventist Church: First, the prophetic roots or the events prophesied in Revelation 10. Second, the prophetic identity defined in Revelation 12. And third, the prophetic message and mission given in Revelation 14.[11]

The assurance of being the result of a biblical prophecy is an enormous blessing for Seventh-day Adventists. It was God who brought this people to existence. And such certainty of our prophetic roots should naturally lead us to obey the command that was given in the same chapter that offers us so much assurance of the divine leading. God told John, who in the vision represented us: "Thou must prophesy again before many peoples, and nations, and tongues, and kings" (Rev. 10:11, KJV).

Secondly, the Bible offers an important description of God's people as "those who keep God's commands and hold fast their testimony about Jesus" (Rev. 12:17). Although there are some churches that keep the Sabbath and others that affirm they have the testimony of Jesus (the spirit of prophecy, according to Rev. 19:10), the Seventh-day Adventist Church alone matches the two characteristics given here.[12]

And finally, a powerful third reason to be an Adventist is that God has entrusted us with a unique message to the world, as described in Revelation 14:6-12. This third characteristic also has a strong link with mission: "The three angels of Revelation 14 represent the people who accept the light of God's messages and go forth as His agents to sound the warning throughout the length and breadth of the earth." [13]

## Disappointed because of the problems within the church

I have met many sincere Adventists who, on the realization that a particular preacher or leader they admired fell into sin, they left the church. More than one very talented pastor has quit ministry in order to birth their own church besides the Seventh-day Adventist Church, disappointed at the failures they have seen in the structure or in some church administrator. This book has also pointed out several issues we need to correct as individuals and as a church as well. Would it all be worth leaving the church?

John the Apostle is given a vision of "someone like a son of man," someone who describes himself as "the First and the Last. I am the Living One; I was dead, and now look, I am alive for ever and ever! And I hold the keys of death and Hades" (Rev. 1:13, 18). The evidence is strong that such character is Jesus Christ Himself. What grabs my attention is that Jesus is portrayed here as walking in the midst of seven candlesticks or lampstands (v. 13).

Verse 20 identifies the seven lampstands with God's church as a whole, so from the first time I read it, that text touched my heart and hit me home. I'm thrilled to remember that Jesus walks in the midst of His church, especially when I spot failures within our denomination. And I believe that thinking of this fact can provide a tremendous hope for you as well. No matter how awfully disappointed you might be for the problems you've seen within the church, you can be assured that Jesus walks among the candlesticks. He watches over His church. He has certainly noticed the problems you spotted, and many more. And even so, He loves His church and walks among us.

Jesus tirelessly watches over His church, to see whether the light of any of His sentinels is burning dim or going out. The church is so imperfect that "if the candlesticks were left to mere human care, the flickering flame would languish and die," but as a church we don't depend upon our own merits or our own strength. Jesus Christ "is the true watchman in the Lord's house, the true warden of the temple courts. His continued care and sustaining grace are the source of life and light."[14]

God knows all those defects you might have spotted in the church and yet He does not forsake her. Instead of rejecting the church because of her very many mistakes, Jesus gave His own life for the church. He will continue to work day and night so that His church will reflect His character. Christ's death will not be in vain, because when He was hung on the cross he did it in order to present her to Himself "as a radiant church, without stain or wrinkle or any other blemish, but holy and blameless" (Eph. 5:27). The Bible clearly says that God "will not reject his people; he will never forsake his inheritance" (Ps. 94:14).

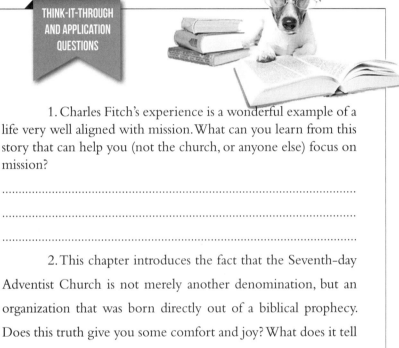

**THINK-IT-THROUGH AND APPLICATION QUESTIONS**

1. Charles Fitch's experience is a wonderful example of a life very well aligned with mission. What can you learn from this story that can help you (not the church, or anyone else) focus on mission?

..............................................................................................

..............................................................................................

..............................................................................................

2. This chapter introduces the fact that the Seventh-day Adventist Church is not merely another denomination, but an organization that was born directly out of a biblical prophecy. Does this truth give you some comfort and joy? What does it tell you?

..............................................................................................

..............................................................................................

..............................................................................................

## References for this chapter

[1] Allan Machado. (2013). From the parking garage to the platform (Unpublished doctoral dissertation). Andrews University, Berrien Springs, MI, p. 109, 110.

[2] James the apostle uses the word "angels" (ἄγγελος), or messengers (James 2:25), to describe the Israelites who went to Jericho as spies and were supposed to come back to the camp with a message. The same expression is used to describe some disciples who Jesus used as His messengers in Samaria (Luke 9:52).

[3]William H. Shea explains that some theologians believe the angel of Rev. 10 is simply an angel and cannot possibly be Jesus because (1) Revelation does not portray Jesus like an angel anywyere else and (2) the use of an oath by God himself is inappropriate. Shea adds, however, that these two reason could even be part of the argument to identify Jesus as the "angel" of Rev. 10, since there are instances in the Old Testament where God is said to have taken oaths (Shea cites Ex. 6:8; Num. 14:30; Eze. 20:15, 28 as examples), and also the figure of Michael in Rev. 12 is angelic and refers to Christ. See William H. Shea. The mighty angel and his message. In Frank B. Holbrook, ed. *Symposium on Revelation – Book 1,* pp. 279-326. Silver Spring, MD: Biblical Research Institute, 1992.

[4]Ellen White. *Christ triumphant,* p. 344.

[5]"This time, which the Angel declares with a solemn oath, is not the end of this world's history, neither of probationary time, but of prophetic time, which would precede the advent of our Lord. That is, the people will not have another message upon definite time. After this period of time, reaching from 1842 to 1844, there can be no definite tracing of the prophetic time. The longest reckoning reaches to the autumn of 1844." Ellen White, *Christ Triumphant,* p. 346.

[6]The 1260-day prophecy of Dan. 12:7 and 9 finds its fulfillment from the year A.D. 538 to 1798, and the 2300-prophecy ends in 1844. The following period is labeled "the time of the end," on the basis of references coming from Dan. 11:40; 12:4, 9.

[7]Ellen White, *Great Controversy,* 356.

[8]LeRoy Edwin Froom. *The prophetic faith of our fathers.* Washington, DC: Review and Herald, 1954, vol. 4, p. 545.

[9]Ranko Stefanovic. *Revelation of Jesus Christ.* Berrien Springs, MI: Andrews University Press, 2002, p. 332.

[10]Scholars have not yet agreed whether the word ἐπί (translated in Rev. 10:11 as "about") means that the church shouls preach about many "peoples, nations, languages and kings," or perhaps the church should focus on preaching to them, rather than "about" them. However, the language of Rev. 10:11's context is very similar to that of Rev. 14:6 ("nation, tribe, language and people"), and it is evidently another reference to the Great Commission, because the message should be preached to "all nations" (Matt. 28:20), "into all the world," and "to all creation" (Mark16:15).

[11]James Nix, A Unique Prophetic Movement. Adventist World. http://www.adventistworld.org/article/559/resources/english/issue-2009-1006/a-unique-prophetic-movement.

[12]Ibid.

[13]Ellen White, *Counsels for the Church,* p. 58.

[14]Ellen White, *Acts of the Apostles,* 586.

BSOLUTELY! And we should. In fact, it's extremely urgent that we escape. We cannot afford to continue swinging back and forth between success and failure like there is no way out. You and I need to realize that God is able to take us out of our miserable situation. But how?

When God created Elizabeth, He wasn't expecting her to be forever condemned to oscillate between sin and repentance. William's struggle with weight gain and dieting and his painful heart attack in the basketball court were not part of God's ideal plan for him. Jesus suffers when he watches people like Cristy do their best to quit smoking, only to backslide into it time and time again. Michael's seemingly-endless fight against his unwanted sexual urges is as heart-wrenching for God as it is for Michael. The Savior cries with Mary as she suffers the impact of her husband's alcohol addiction.

But God does not just cry with us. He's got a powerful answer to all of those problems. When Jesus died on that horrible cross some twenty centuries ago, He did so with mission in mind. He wants to set us free from every single thing that enslaves us. God wants to set us free from sin so we can spend eternity with Him. And the Bible declares that very soon Jesus will see the fruit of his hard work and He will "be satisfied" (Is. 53:11).

What a blessed hope! When Jesus comes again, everything will be new. You won't have to keep struggling with your weaknesses anymore. There will be no more oscillation. No more suffering in the rocking chair of life. But in the meantime, how will we be able to get out of the rocking chair?

As we have seen, Paul the Apostle cried for help in a similar situation: "What a wretched man I am! Who will rescue me from this body that is subject to death?" (Rom. 7:24). By ourselves, we will never be able overcome our cycle of oscillation between success and failure. The more you try to do good, the more you will realize you can't do it by yourself. You are a prisoner of sin, no matter how much you try to deny it. Deep inside your heart, you want to do God's will. But it's like something inside of you is waging war against your intentions to follow God's lead.

At times you might feel like you can't take it anymore, but there is hope. There's no reason to give up. All that needs to happen is that you turn to Jesus and give your heart to Him. Unless you and I recognize we can't do anything by ourselves to solve the issue, we'll never get it fixed. But if we allow Him, God will make our most precious dreams come true.

He will change our hearts, our structure, from the inside out. We'll get a brand new heart that is aligned with mission. The Bible clearly says that "if anyone is in Christ, the new creation has come: The old has gone, the new is here!" (2 Cor. 5:17). Jesus Christ our Lord "is able to keep you from stumbling and to present you before his glorious presence without fault and with great joy" (Jude 1:24).

But until that glorious day when Jesus comes back, you'll have to be constantly watching out to make sure everything you do is aligned with mission. You were not created merely to grow up, earn a degree, have a family, make money, and then die. You were created for mission. You were created to glorify God's name, and to bring others to Him, so that every tongue will "acknowledge that Jesus Christ is Lord, to the glory of God the Father" (Phil. 2:11).

Every morning, plan ahead so that your decisions are consistent with what you were created for. Throughout the day, ask yourself whether or not you're bringing glory to God by the way you're living. Ask yourself whether you're bringing others to Jesus. And if you find out that you're doing stuff that won't bring glory to God and won't bring anyone to the feet of the cross, then it's time to give that up.

Turn your eyes upon Jesus, and everything else will grow dim as you focus on Him. Your weaknesses, whatever they might be, will start fading away as Christ takes over. You'll be able to say, like the Apostle, "I have been crucified with Christ and I no longer live, but

Christ lives in me. The life I now live in the body, I live by faith in the Son of God, who loved me and gave himself for me" (Gal. 2:20).

As a church, we also need to realign our structure to mission, from the local church with its individual members to the General Conference with its regional Divisions. Healing the sick is good, but that's not the church's mission. It makes sense to establish educational institutions and church buildings, but we should not allow those projects to eat up all of our resources and distract us from mission.

Church members need to make mission-oriented decisions like making more friends and praying for them until they surrender to Jesus' love. Every single church member needs to get involved in some sort of ministry according to their gifts. If your pastor and other local leaders don't ask for your help, you still have the responsibility of doing something in order to bring others to Christ. You don't have to stand in front of everybody to preach or go door-knocking every Sabbath at 3 pm if you don't feel like it. But you have to ask yourself, what is it that I'm good at? What can I do for Christ? How can I reach others and bring them closer to Jesus?

On the other hand, we the pastors need to be willing to pay the price of shepherding church members instead of merely babysitting them. We need to do everything in our hands to focus on mission, both locally and globally. Most of the budget for our churches should be allocated for mission, not for mere maintenance (even if we find it hard to convince the church board). Most of our time should be spent in making disciples, not merely featuring programs, holding committee meetings and fighting fires of wrangling among the saints.

At the different organizational levels of the church, leaders need to be constantly evaluating the way church business is conducted, so that we are really focused on mission. It won't be easy, and it won't happen overnight. But if we're intentional, God will lead us there.

More emphasis should be placed on the importance of offerings, so local members don't get the idea that tithing is enough. More missionaries should be sent to underprivileged places such as the 10/40 Window. Missionaries should be sent to do mission, not merely to hold teaching or administrative positions. Mission projects should be more focused on reaching the unreached than in "building" the church where it already exists. Official statistical reports need to better represent our intentional efforts in reaching those people groups that have never heard the gospel, and making disciples among them.

By God's grace, today I choose that I'm not going to stay idle in my rocking chair hoping that the General Conference will come up with a great idea and implement it. I'm not going to keep swinging back and forth in my pew-style rocking chair expecting the pastor to preach a his best sermon every week and bring great musicians and a nice guest speaker every now and then.

I'll just move away from the rocking chair and offer my assistance in the different ministries of my congregation. I'll increase my faithfulness in tithe and offerings, and I'll do my best to befriend others and bring them to the feet of Jesus. And I'll pray for Jesus, who walks among the candlesticks, to do whatever's left so my fellow church members, the pastor and the other leaders, will better align their lives and even church.

Want to do some follow-up to this book through sermons, workshops,

and small group meetings? Need books in boxes at discount prices?

Email us for free PowerPoint and PDF stuff,

or for bulk purchases:

editor@escapefromtherockingchair.com

Check us out on the Web:

# www.escapefromtherockingchair.com